Vietnam Stories
I Never Told

Vietnam Stories I Never Told

Memoir of an Infantryman at the Cambodian Border, 1968–1969

HERBERT G. JANSEN

McFarland & Company, Inc., Publishers
Jefferson, North Carolina

Library of Congress Cataloging-in-Publication Data

Names: Jansen, Herbert G., 1948– author.
Title: Vietnam stories I never told : memoir of an infantryman at the Cambodian border, 1968–1969 / Herbert G. Jansen.
Other titles: Memoir of an infantryman at the Cambodian border, 1968–1969
Description: Jefferson, North Carolina : McFarland & Company, Inc., Publishers, 2025. | "Corp Tactical Zone III". | Includes bibliographical references and index.
Identifiers: LCCN 2025001478 | ISBN 9781476697611 (paperback : acid free paper) ∞
ISBN 9781476655338 (ebook)
Subjects: LCSH: Jansen, Herbert G., 1948– | Vietnam War, 1961–1975—Personal narratives, American—Juvenile literature. | United States. Army. Infantry Regiment, 9th. Battalion, 4th Company A—Biography. | Soldiers—United States—Biography. | Vietnam War, 1961–1975—Campaigns. | Stamford (Conn.)—Biography.
Classification: LCC DS559.5 .J367 2025 | DDC 959.704/342 [B]—dc23/eng/20250207
LC record available at https://lccn.loc.gov/2025001478

ISBN (print) 978-1-4766-9761-1
ISBN (ebook) 978-1-4766-5533-8

© 2025 Herbert G. Jansen. All rights reserved

No part of this book may be reproduced or transmitted in any form or by any means, electronic or mechanical, including photocopying or recording, or by any information storage and retrieval system, without permission in writing from the publisher.

Front cover images: author in front of the Manchu EM Club in Tay Ninh, March 1968; envelope of a letter sent home during deployment; author's dog tags.

Printed in the United States of America

McFarland & Company, Inc., Publishers
 Box 611, Jefferson, North Carolina 28640
 www.mcfarlandpub.com

For all the Manchus of the 4/9th Battalion
of the 25th Infantry Division who served in Vietnam,
many of whom gave their lives or suffered wounds
serving their country and helping
and protecting their Manchu brothers.

Table of Contents

Acknowledgments	ix
Preface	1
1. "There's a shadow hanging over me"	5
2. "I was a boy you had to keep busy"	9
3. Infantry Bound	18
4. Hello, Vietnam	26
5. My M-16 Rifle	38
6. The Manchus	45
7. Saddle Up	50
8. The 1968 Presidential Campaign	53
9. The Assassination of Martin Luther King, Jr.	57
10. Leadership	60
11. The Monsoon Season	65
12. The May Offensive	75
13. The Longest Month of My Life	82
14. May Finally Ends	95
15. Attrition Warfare	101
16. The Assassination of Robert F. Kennedy	111
17. Phase II of Operation Toan Thang	114
18. Friendship	120

Table of Contents

19. The August Offensive	127
20. The Silver Star	131
21. Rest and Relaxation	136
22. Bereavement Leave	146
23. Short Timer	158
Afterword	163
Reflections	168
Chapter Notes	171
Index	177

Acknowledgments

I would like to acknowledge the support and encouragement I have received while writing this book. My thanks go to the following.

To my wife, Anne Morris Swope, who was my inspiration for the book. I shared many of my stories with her after reading the letters and she convinced me to share my story. Without her encouragement I never would have written this book. And she was really my co-author. I wrote all the stories and she edited and also did extensive research and writing on many of the topics in the book. I thank her from the bottom of my heart for her support.

To my daughter, Rachel Delevante, and my grandsons, who fill my heart with joy. Rachel told me, as she was reading the book, that she thought "he is not going to make it" but then thought "oh, but he did." When she finished reading the book, she sent me socks.

With deep gratitude I thank Michael Walzer, professor emeritus at the Institute of Advanced Study, author and political theorist, and Judith Walzer, professor of literature and academic administrator. I am honored that they read my book and I am thankful for their invaluable feedback and advice.

To Dwight Davis, my dear friend and amazing squad leader from the Manchus, who read my draft and provided support and encouragement. I thank him for his friendship and support and I thank his wife Gloria for the same and for finding me on the internet so I could reconnect with Dwight and get to know Gloria and their family after so many years had passed.

To John Ludvigsen, my cousin, who was a career Air Force officer,

Acknowledgments

and spent his military career in intelligence, rising to the rank of major before he retired. We grew up together and have been great friends throughout our lives. John read and reread many drafts of my book and offered support, recommendations, and, very importantly, encouragement. After he read the first draft he told me he wished the book would never end.

To James M. Arrison, U.S. Navy captain (retired), Anne's uncle and godfather. He served in Vietnam from 1966 to 1968 as captain of a Swift boat patrolling off the coast of Na Trang. He read and reread my drafts and provided support and encouragement that my story was worth telling.

To Jonathan S. Swope, U.S. Marine Corp. lt. colonel (retired), my brother-in-law. His encouragement was very important to me, especially coming from a career Marine with multiple tours in Afghanistan and Iraq. And to Cynthia Bater, my sister-in-law, who provided helpful feedback and a different, valuable point of view.

To Steve and Anne Hoffman, two dear friends from my days in the accounting profession. Their encouragement and enthusiasm kept us focused. Since Steve and I worked together for so many years he can attest to the fact that these are stories I never told, until now.

To Ron and Susanna Lokos, my good friends and neighbors, who over the years read and reread drafts of my book and have been so supportive, especially in those moments when I doubted myself, doubted if my story would really be of interest to others.

And finally, to Joe Abbatiello, my good friend and neighbor. We talked about the book, and the revisions I was making, summer after summer, over a scotch on his deck. I appreciate his continued interest and support.

Preface

The year I served in Vietnam was the most influential year of my life. I arrived at the Ben Hoa Air Base in Vietnam on March 13, 1968, and boarded the freedom plane home on March 10, 1969. In 1968, almost 17,000 American troops were killed[1] and more than 87,000 were wounded,[2] an astonishing number of casualties, far exceeding any other year of the war.

When my father died, we found a box full of letters I wrote during my first eighteen months of active duty, including the year I spent in Vietnam. Reading the letters, I was reminded of the amazing relationship I had with my parents, and I long for them now that they are gone. I was reminded of how I tried to protect them from what I was going through when I was in Vietnam, with a few minor instances where I seemed to lose sight of that goal.

I was also overwhelmed by the memories the letters invoked of my service in Vietnam, memories I had never shared with anyone. I started telling these stories to my family—the easier ones to tell, anyway. I held the hard ones back for a long time. The first telling of each story was so vivid, the second telling, less so. I learned that when a traumatic event is repeatedly brought to conscious awareness and recalled, a person's memory of the event fades. So I started to write. Fifteen years later, I am finally finished writing. Some of the stories were hard to tell.

During the Vietnam War many young men residing in the United States were asked to serve their country in the military. Some fulfilled their military commitment by enlisting in the National Guard,

Preface

Coast Guard or Army Reserves. Some joined ROTC programs and attended military academies and later went to Vietnam as officers. Some enlisted or were drafted after finishing high school or, in some cases, college.

Some young men received deferments (or delays) from the draft because they were attending college. Some obtained exemptions from the draft for medical reasons. Some went to jail or left the country to avoid the draft. Some went unwillingly, unable to obtain a reprieve. We all came at the issue from a different perspective. We all made the best decision we could at the time.

Those men who graduated from programs like ROTC or the military academies like West Point or the Naval Academy, and then entered the military bound for Vietnam, were educated on the political and ideological bases for the war. However, most young men who served in Vietnam had little knowledge about why the war was being waged other than some vague notion that we needed to stop the spread of communism. I was one of these. The song "Hello Vietnam" sung by Johnny Wright provides a fair description of the way many of us understood America's participation in the war between North Vietnam and South Vietnam: "We must save freedom now at any cost, or someday our own freedom will be lost."[3]

In Vietnam, I believe most of the villagers cared more about the village political structure than the national structure. I believe many of the Vietnamese who sided with one side or the other, south or north, did so based on how they had been treated as opposed to a deep view on the form of the national government. I believe many South Vietnamese people thought we were occupiers, not liberators.

My story is not to justify the war or my service or to question the decisions of others. This is just my story. The story of a non-political young man facing the draft and accepting it for a variety of reasons. Those I served with may have slightly different or even very different recollections. I understand that. My story is told from my eyes and my memory. They say memories are complicated and contradictory in stressful situations.[4] I believe that.

Later in my life I had the opportunity to talk to a mountain

Preface

climber who reached the summit of Mount Everest as part of a team. When her team reunited years later they were amazed at how different their recollections were of the major events that occurred on the climb. I was not surprised.

My story is also a narrow one, about my squad, my platoon. We were often in the line of fire and we had to help each other stay alive. I knew very little about what was happening in the other platoons in our company, even though at times they were operating twenty or thirty yards away from us. I knew very little about what has happening in the other companies in our battalion or about our battalion's role in the various operations we participated in. I knew almost nothing about what was happening in other parts of Vietnam.

The war I experienced in Vietnam was not like the experiences of the characters in many of the books that have been written or the movies that have been made about the Vietnam War. Borrowing from Walter Cronkite's televised commentary on February 27, 1968, the Vietnam War I experienced was a war fought by young and honorable men, asked by their country to defend democracy, who did the best they could.

Chapter 1

"There's a shadow hanging over me"

In the summer of 1967, I was working as a switchman, officially known as a central office repairman, for the Southern New England Telephone Company. I was 19 years old. I had a red 1963 Chevy Impala Super Sport two-door hardtop with a black interior, a 1966 Triumph Bonneville motorcycle, and a terrific girlfriend.

I really liked cars, motorcycles, music, and girls. My grandfather gave me my first car when I was 16 years old, a dark blue 1951 Ford two-door sedan. One day my friend Paul and I decided to rebuild the engine, so we pulled the engine out of the car with a chain over the rafter of the garage and took it apart piece by piece. By the time my father realized what was happening there were hundreds of parts lying on the garage floor.

"What are you doing?"

"Rebuilding the engine."

"There was nothing wrong with the engine."

"I know, we just thought it would be a good idea to rebuild it. It will run better."

"Hmmm ... hopefully it will still run."

I sold my Triumph and bought a virtually new Harley Davidson Sportster XLH for $500. It had only 50 miles on it but had been in a garage that had caught fire and it was burnt to a crisp. My father walked by the garage when I first brought it home and shook his head. He was pretty impressed, though, after I took it apart, cleaned all the pieces, rebuilt it, replaced the wiring, and had it professionally painted

Vietnam Stories I Never Told

Herbert G. Jansen on his Triumph Bonneville motorcycle in 1967.

and re-chromed. It was red with a black lace overlay and a fat whitewall tire on the back.

In those days, if I was home, I was in the garage working on the car or the motorcycle, and if I wasn't at home or at work, I was in my car. I loved the radio, I loved rock and roll, and I loved parking at the beach with my girl.

Life was pretty good for me then except I knew I was going to be drafted; I just didn't know how soon. I was young and healthy, and I was not attending college. No one in my family had ever attended college. I never even thought about going to college. We all thought people went to college because they couldn't find a job. My girlfriend wanted to get married, but I just wasn't ready. She was too young, and I still had other girls on my mind. Getting drafted and going to Vietnam was inevitable. It didn't bother me too much, though. I had been raised to believe military service was an obligation.

1. "There's a shadow hanging over me"

One day in July 1967 I drove down to the draft board in Stamford to see if they knew when I was going to be drafted. The Beatles' song "Yesterday" came on the radio. You can't help but feel melancholy when you hear this song. On that day, though, some of the lines really hit home, especially the line "there's a shadow hanging over me."[1] I had the shadow of Vietnam hanging over me and I felt like I just needed to go and get it over with.

Some of my friends enlisted in the Marines directly after high school and were already headed for Vietnam. The four-year commitment they were making did not appeal to me at the time. Four years seemed like an eternity then. I found out later, too late, that there was a two-year option.

The clerk at the draft board said, based on the number of guys being drafted from Connecticut each month, I'd be drafted in January or February (1968), maybe sooner. "Could you just take me now?"

I received orders to report to the Stamford train station on September 26, 1967, for the trip to New Haven for induction, and then on to Fort Dix in New Jersey for basic training. I started paying more attention to the news then, and the news was pretty bad, I realized. The only paper I ever read was the local newspaper, *The Stamford Advocate*. We only had one television, a black-and-white set in the living room. I was accustomed to hearing the evening news broadcast in the background when my mom and dad were watching. Sometimes I would sit with them and watch. I was accustomed to hearing about what was going on in Vietnam, about the number of troops killed and wounded each day. I hadn't really focused on what was going on here in the United States. The riots in Philadelphia, Boston, Cincinnati, Atlanta, Buffalo, Newark, Plainfield, Detroit, and Los Angeles seemed as distant to me as Vietnam.

In November 1966 Stephen Stills wrote the song "For What It's Worth."[2] Buffalo Springfield recorded the song a few days later and the single was released before the end of the year. The song reached Number 7 on the Billboard Hot 100 by the spring of 1967. We all thought the song was about the war in Vietnam, but the song was actually about curfew and loitering ordinances being imposed in Los Angeles.

When the song was written, Buffalo Springfield was a cover band for a club on the Sunset Strip where curfew and loitering ordinances were being enforced. The social and political unrest at the time, and the different views of wrong and right, stretched from coast to coast.

The summer of 1967 was called the "Long Hot Summer." Riots erupted across the United States. The worst was in Detroit, later referred to as "The Great Rebellion," where a confrontation between Black residents and the Detroit Police Department escalated significantly when the governor of Michigan sent in the Michigan National Guard and President Johnson sent in the United States Army's 82nd and 101st Airborne divisions. After five days of rioting in Detroit there were 43 people dead, almost 1,200 injured, 7,200 arrests, and more than 2,000 buildings burned to the ground.

Ironically, the summer of 1967 was also the "Summer of Love." Over 100,000 people, mostly kids my age, flocked to the San Francisco Bay area, mostly to the city neighborhood of Haight-Ashbury. They started arriving in early spring and stayed there, and more just kept coming. The song "San Francisco (Be Sure to Wear Flowers in Your Hair)"[3] is often credited with bringing them there. The song was written by John Phillips (of the Mamas & the Papas) and sung by Scott McKenzie to promote the Monterey International Pop Festival. The song hit the top of the Billboard 100 in no time. I think the song was a welcome respite from the riots going on across the United States, and the backdrop of the Vietnam War.

Chapter 2

"I was a boy you had to keep busy"

I was born in Brooklyn, New York, in 1948. Both my mother and father were first-generation Americans. All four of my grandparents were born in Norway and immigrated to the United States through Ellis Island at the turn of the twentieth century, and settled down in Brooklyn where both of my parents were born. I never knew my paternal grandparents, but I lived with my maternal grandparents for most of my youth. In those days, and perhaps particularly because they were immigrants, multiple generations of family lived together or nearby.

My father, George, was born in 1918 in Brooklyn. When he was eight years old, his parents had saved enough to buy a small farm in Vineland, New Jersey. His mother, Thora, worked the farm while his father, Adolf, commuted to Brooklyn to work scraping (refinishing) hardwood floors.

In those days hardwood floors were refinished by hand. They call it "push-scraping." My grandfather worked on his knees with a tool that looked like a plane for woodworking. The plane had a horizontal handle, perpendicular to the base, so it could be held with two hands, and a blade about two inches wide. Starting at his knees with the blade of the plane on the floor, he would push down and out until his body was extended over the floor, taking a sliver of wood off the floor in the process. He did this over and over until the entire room was scraped except the edges. Then he used a hand scraper to scrape the edges.

A hand scraper is a smaller tool that has a special kind of handle and a blade that faces the floor at a 45-degree angle. To hand scrape the edges, the tool is positioned against the wall and pulled back with the dominant hand while applying pressure to the blade with the other, taking a sliver of wood off each time. My father said my grandfather could do one arm push-ups all day long.

My grandparents lost the farm in New Jersey in foreclosure after the stock market crash of 1929 and moved back to Brooklyn. Soon after, in the early 1930s, my grandfather bought an electric belt sander. Even though the belt sander was difficult to handle and required a lot of strength, the physical difficulty of refinishing hard wood floors was greatly diminished. Advertisements for the belt sander boasted "One man on his feet is worth six on their knees."

By then, my grandfather had made a name for himself in Brooklyn as a floor scraper and he taught my father how to scrap floors at a very young age. That was a good thing, because my grandfather passed away in 1934 when my father was 16 years old. My father took over responsibility for supporting his mother, sister, and himself, scraping floors.

Although my father knew how to scrape floors when his father died, he didn't know how to get jobs. He decided to make up business cards from paper cutouts that said "George Jansen, Experienced Floor Scraper" and left them at every paint store in Brooklyn he could find. Soon he had enough work to support his family and a few years later he was able to buy an electric edger. Although he used the electric belt sander and edger, which made him more productive and allowed him to earn more, his ability to hand scrape gave him a certain stature in the flooring community. If a person knew how to use a hand scraper, that meant he was a "real" floor scraper.

Historically, floor sanders and refinishers were referred to as floor scrapers. That comes from the time when there were no sanding machines and all the work to prepare the floor was done with scrapers. The craftsman in the trade continued to call themselves floor scrapers well after the introduction of sanding machines. My father always referred to himself as a floor scraper.

After arriving in the United States, my maternal grandfather, Anskar, worked on barges moving goods along the Hudson River

2. "I was a boy you had to keep busy"

in New York. My grandmother, Agnes, cleaned houses. My mother, Doris, was born in Brooklyn in 1921 and her brother, Herbert, was born in 1925. Later, during the early years of the Depression, they had to give up their small apartment because they couldn't afford the rent any longer. My mother and Herbert went to live with relatives, while my grandfather lived on a barge and my grandmother lived in the home of a family that she cleaned for. Several years later when my grandfather became the captain of his barge, they were able to afford a small apartment again and the family was reunited. My grandfather still lived primarily on the barge, though.

In 1938, my maternal grandfather and his brother bought a brownstone in Brooklyn. His brother and his brother's wife and children, Harry, Kenny and Helen, lived on the first floor, and my grandparents, my mother, and Herbert lived on the second floor. My mother and father met and married in 1941. My father moved into the second-floor apartment in the brownstone with my grandparents and continued to support his mother and sister in their apartment nearby. My older sister Carole and I were both born while they resided in that second-floor apartment.

My father joined the Army in October 1942, and served until December 1945. After basic training he boarded a troop ship bound for England where he spent the better part of a year along the English Channel. There he received specialized training as a tugboat engineer and a crane operator, and assisted in preparation for the Normandy invasion by American, British, and Canadian forces on June 6, 1944. During the invasion he was involved in moving troops to the beachheads, and soon after he was sent to France, moving supplies from the ships that crossed the English Channel bound for the front. Although they regularly selected men from his company to be reassigned to the front, he was never selected.

My father's favorite war story (told at least a thousand times) was about when he was a tugboat engineer. Just after he joined a tugboat crew as an engineer they were out at sea in the English Channel when the tugboat's engine suddenly failed. The captain told my father to go down to the engine room and get the engine running. He went down to the engine room and looked around for a while without a clue of what to do, and eventually saw a big red button that said "press to restart engine." He pressed the button and the engine restarted. When he went back up to the bridge the captain asked him what was wrong. My father said it was just a simple thing that took him no time to resolve. The captain slapped him on the back and said he was a master engineer, and after that the entire crew treated him like a king. I can still hear his laugh when he gets to that part. He loved that story.

My mother's brother Herbert enlisted in the Army in the summer of 1943 and shipped out to Italy after basic training. He was killed just a few days after arriving there, on November 8, 1943. He was only 18. He was posthumously awarded the Purple Heart "For Military Merit

George H. Jansen, Herb's father, in Army fatigues sometime between 1942 and 1945 (World War II).

2. "I was a boy you had to keep busy"

and for Wounds Received in Action resulting in his death" on December 18, 1943.

After Herbert's death my grandfather quit his job on the barge so he could be with my grandmother and my mother, and he began installing tin ceilings to make a living. My grandfather and grandmother, and my mother, too, I think, never really recovered from Herbert's death. A letter my mother sent to Herbert after he shipped out came back unopened, stamped "Deceased." They already knew by then, of course. After my mother passed away, we found that letter in the box with my letters from Vietnam, unopened, just the way she received it back all those years ago.

My grandfather's religious devotion intensified after Herbert was killed. I think he turned to God to help him cope with the loss of his son, and he wanted to help others find God too. He became a minister at St. Matthew's–Emanuel Lutheran Church in Park Slope, Brooklyn, New York, and also ran a Red Cross soup kitchen nearby. He and my grandmother moved into an apartment above the church when my parents moved us to Valley Stream, Long Island, when I was two years old.

I remember going to church in Brooklyn every Sunday to see my grandparents and hear my grandfather's sermons. The parishioners of his church were a mixture of immigrants and Blacks who would

Herbert S. Knudsen, Herb's uncle, in Army dress uniform before shipping out in the summer of 1943 (World War II).

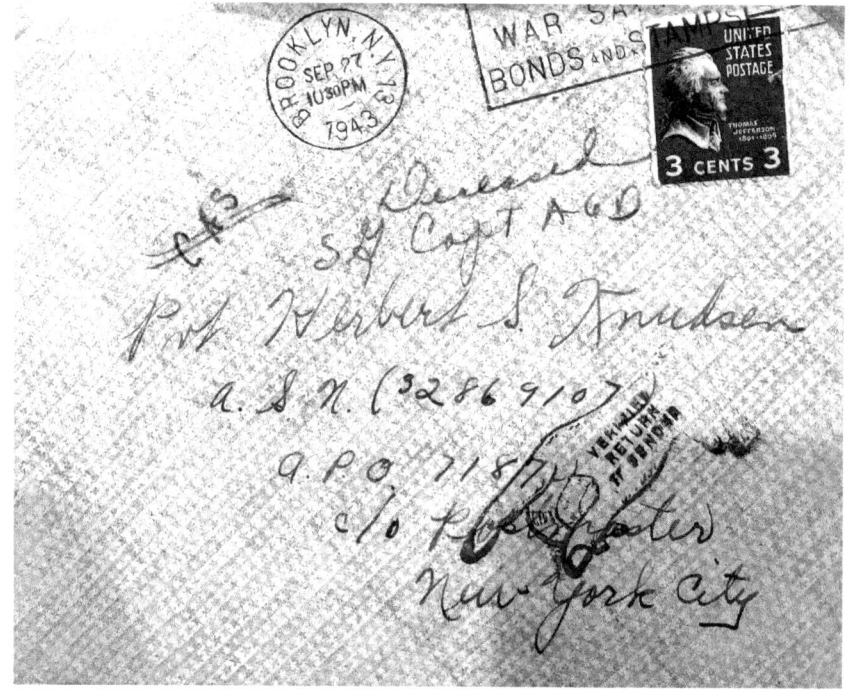

Letter sent to Herbert S. Knudsen, Herb's uncle, September 27, 1943, returned marked "Deceased."

sing and pray with fervor, just as my grandfather did in leading their prayers. There were times when it felt like the whole building was shaking from their collective intensity. Many Sundays my sister Carole and I would spend the entire day at the church.

My grandparents had a huge impact on my life. They were kind and caring and had a way of living in our house with us but also apart, allowing my parents to run the house as their own. One unimportant detail has stuck with me my whole life: my grandfather always wore a suit. He had almost no money and probably owned one or maybe two suits but he always looked dapper. In his later years before his health failed, he made several trips to Norway and gave sermons at churches around his home town.

2. "I was a boy you had to keep busy"

We lived in Valley Stream for six years or so, close to my Aunt Ester and her family. Aunt Ester was my mother's first cousin. Aunt Ester's son John (mentioned in my letters) and I are very close in age, and we got into a lot of trouble together during those formative years. Aunt Ester used to tether John to a tree so he wouldn't wander off. After I painted my bedroom red, my mother wondered if she should have tied me to a tree as well. We also lived close to my aunt ("Tante") Josephine, my father's sister, and her five boys (including Gary, the youngest, mentioned in my letters). I spent many weeks and weekends with them.

My younger sister, Kristine, was born while we lived in Valley Stream. I was around four years old at the time. People talk about older siblings being jealous when younger siblings are born. I never understood that. The day I saw my mother and Aunt Ester oohing and ahhing at my little sister in the crib was the best day of my life up until then. I knew they would never pay attention to me again and I would be free!

My first-grade teacher told my mother I was a boy you had to keep busy. I think that was true then and is still true today. They say so much of who we are, who we will become, is established or already evident in those early formative years. I am still impressed by my first-grade teacher's insight.

When I was around eight years old, we moved to Stamford, Connecticut. We rented a house in the Cove, right on the Long Island Sound, and my father bought us an old rowboat with a small outboard engine that we kept tied up in a bay just feet from the Sound. How idyllic my young life was then. A few years later my parents bought a house on Courtland Avenue, not far from the Cove and my grandparents left Brooklyn and moved in with us, into an apartment my father crafted for them on the second floor of the house. My grandfather died while I was still in high school, and just a few years later, my grandmother died while I was in Vietnam.

Just as my grandfather taught my father how to scrape floors, my father taught me. I started helping my father scrape floors when I was 14 years old. In the beginning I just carried stuff and fetched things when he needed them, but as soon as I was strong enough, he taught me how to run the edger and the sanding machine. By the time I was 18 I was producing just as much as the old timers and earned the same hourly rate.

I consider myself very lucky to have had the chance to work with my father. I saw him in his work life and understood what he did every day. There was no security in his work except his reputation as a hard worker and he had to produce every day to keep his job.

The work my father did was very hard, and he was a taskmaster on the job. When he said do something, no matter what I was doing I dropped everything and did what he said. I am still like that, to a fault, my wife says. There were weeks, even months, in Vietnam when we moved every day on foot, covering as much as ten klicks (short for kilometers) a day through rice patties and jungle while carrying over fifty pounds of gear in the blistering heat, and we had to dig foxholes or build small bunkers every night when we got to our assigned locations. Some of the guys would complain about having to dig and fill sandbags after ten hours of humping through the jungle or rice paddies. I would laugh to myself. It was much easier than working with my father.

I was a typical teenager, typical for the times anyway. We used to hang out at Mazza's Confectionery Store on Main Street. Mazza's had a luncheonette counter, and that is where we all gathered. Most of my friends were Italian. We formed a gang and called ourselves "The Sicilians." We even had jackets made with "The Sicilians" printed across the front. No one seemed to care that I was as blond and blue eyed as anyone could possibly be (and definitely not Sicilian). We didn't have a purpose; we just wanted to be a gang. It was really just about dating girls and listening to music and driving cars.

I attended J.D. Wright Tech High School initially, rather than regular high school, and learned the electrician trade. One week we wore trade clothes and worked in the shop, the next week we wore slacks and ties and studied academics in a regular classroom. I transferred to Stamford High School for my senior year, mostly because all my friends went there. I never pursued the electrician trade, although

2. "I was a boy you had to keep busy"

the electrical skills I learned have come in handy throughout my life. After I graduated from high school, I went to work for the telephone company where the training from the trade school was both helpful in getting the job and in doing the work.

Chapter 3

Infantry Bound

When I arrived at Fort Dix one of the clerks was conducting interviews to decide if we had any special skills that could determine where we went for training after basic. The clerk asked me what I did in civilian life. I said I was a switchman for the telephone company. He looked switchman up in his book of occupations and switchman wasn't listed. I realized later that my job was probably listed as central office repairman rather than switchman. In any case, I knew I needed to go into the infantry, or I would never hear the end of it from my father. "Could you just put me in the infantry?"

At the recruit arrival center at Fort Dix, New Jersey, the Army had mostly short timers running things. The short timers were guys that had just days or weeks left before being discharged and they were responsible for getting the new recruits their uniforms, haircuts and providing general oversight while we were in the process of being assigned to training companies.

The short timers had the recruits running around in circles and when we arrived they rushed us to change from our civilian clothing to our fatigues and out of the barracks for formation. Many of us, including me, forgot to lock our lockers in the process. Most of us had arrived with some cash and by the time we got back to the barracks the cash was gone. I only fell for that one once.

Basic training was pretty much what I expected. A few things surprised me, like to wake us up in the morning, they rolled metal trashcans down the center of the barracks. Once we got to our training company they worked us really hard and really long. I didn't mind. I

3. Infantry Bound

can still hear the cadences the drill sergeants used to keep us moving along and in step, especially the Jody calls.[1]

> "Used to drive a limousine
>   Now I'm wearing Army green"
>
> "Used to date a beauty queen,
>   Now I date my M-16"
>
> "Ain't no use in looking down
>   Ain't no discharge on the ground"
>
> "Ain't no use in going back,
>   Jody's got your Cadillac"
>
> "Ain't no use in calling home,
>   Jody's got your girl and gone"
>
> "Ain't no use in feeling blue,
>   Jody's got your sister too"[2]

November 7, 1967

Dear Mom and Dad,

We had to fill out papers the other day if we made expert on the firing range, to be sent to the hometown papers so you might be seeing my name in the Advocate *soon.*

I thought things were going to start slowing up a little after we finished firing but I guess I was wrong because we have been busy from 5 in the morning to 7 in the evening every day.

After I finished basic training at Fort Dix, I was sent to Fort Jackson in South Carolina for advanced infantry training (AIT). I'd never been in the South before. I felt really far away from home. They kept us just as busy in AIT as they did in basic, so I didn't have time to write letters.

The air at Fort Jackson, warm and comfortable in December, turned rainy and cold in January. Surprisingly this turned out to be good training for Vietnam. At Fort Jackson we spent most of January and February living outside, and we were wet and cold most of the time. In the Nam, during the rainy season it rained almost every day in the late afternoon, so we would be wet and cold all night.

I was still at Fort Jackson on January 30, 1968, when the Viet Cong ("VC")[3] and the North Vietnamese Army ("NVA")[4] launched the Tet Offensive. The first day of Lunar New Year, Tet, is Vietnam's most important holiday. There was a ceasefire agreement in effect, so the Vietnamese people could celebrate their holiday without fear of being attacked. The VC and NVA attacked anyway. They launched a series of surprise attacks on cities and towns across South Vietnam. The invasion of the U.S. Embassy in Saigon was reported heavily in the news, and was a shock to Americans, who until then believed the United States had the war firmly in hand. This was the most significant military operation undertaken by either side so far in the war. The U.S. and South Vietnamese troops were caught off guard and lost control of several cities and towns, and took weeks to regain control.

The official calendar of Vietnam, the Georgian Calendar, was adopted in 1954. However, the traditional Vietnamese Lunar Calendar still establishes the dates of traditional holidays, including the Lunar New Year, Tet Nguyen Dan, which means "Festival of the First Day" and refers to the beginning of spring.

Lunar calendar days begin and end at midnight, and months begin on the day of the new moon. Lunar Calendar years start on the second or third new moon after the winter solstice (depending on the date of the new moon), so the date of Tet Nguyen Dan varies from year to year.

In 1968, Tet Nguyen Dan (the new year) started on January 31, 1968. However, the celebration began the day before, on January 30, 1968, much like New Year's Eve and New Year's Day are celebrated around the world based on the Georgian Calendar. The Vietnamese holiday is divided into three time periods, though, rather than two time periods, the preparation before Tet (tat nien), the eve of Tet (giao thua) which is when the Kitchen God (Ong Tao) returns to earth, and the day of and days following Tet (tet nien).

Tet is also the shared birthday of all Vietnamese people and is celebrated after midnight on the eve of Tet, so a Vietnamese person's age does not change on the actual date they were born, but rather on the following Tet. Also, when Vietnamese children are born they are already considered to be one year old and so they will turn two years

3. Infantry Bound

old on the Tet following their birth. Such different ways of thinking about life and living, even small things...

The Vietnamese people believe the first visitor that enters their home in the new year determines the family's fortune for the entire year, so no one enters another family's home on the first day without being invited. Being the first person to enter a house in the new year is one of the Vietnamese people's most important customs. If good things come to a family on the first day of the year, the Vietnamese people believe the year ahead will be full of blessings. Families invite someone who they know to be a good person and someone who is successful to be the first to visit their home. Just to be sure nothing goes wrong, sometimes the owner of a home will leave just before midnight and return after the clock strikes twelve just to be certain that no one else who might bring misfortune upon the family can enter the home first.

The first day of Tet is reserved for immediate family. Children wear new clothes and greet their parents and grandparents and receive envelopes of lucky money from them. Although not strictly adhered to, the second day of Tet is usually reserved for visits with friends, and the third day is reserved for visits with teachers, who are held in high regard by the Vietnamese people.

There are many other customs and traditions associated with Tet. Sweeping the floor during Tet is forbidden as doing so symbolizes sweeping away good luck. Anyone who recently experienced a loss of a family member may not visit anyone else during Tet, for fear that such a visit may bring bad luck or even death to those who are visited. This seems harsh but that's the custom.

During the Vietnam War, until 1968, a truce was observed during Tet Nguyen Dan celebrations, recognized by both sides in the conflict. This allowed Vietnamese families to travel freely to visit family and friends for the celebration. In 1968, however, this lull in the fighting against the backdrop of the Tet Nguyen Dan festivities provided cover for the movement of VC troops into and around South Vietnam. Once in place, the VC and NVA, were able to launch a series of surprise attacks against United States and South Vietnamese forces. This series of attacks is named after Tet Nguyen Dan ... the "Tet Offensive."

Vietnam Stories I Never Told

In early December 1967 Gen. Westmoreland began issuing a series of warnings indicating that the NVA and VC were planning an unusual offensive. United States forces were kept on full alert going into the holiday. Gen. Westmoreland tried unsuccessfully to get President Thieu, the president of South Vietnam, to cancel or curtail the Tet Nguyen Dan holiday leave granted for approximately 400,000 Army of the Republic of Vietnam (ARVN) troops. On January 30, 1968, after the initial waves of attacks scattered around the country, President Thieu did finally cancel the holiday leave of his ARVN troops. However, many of them either did not receive the message or were unable to get back to their units before the NVA and VC launched the full force of their planned attacks.

Even though Gen. Westmoreland had anticipated a significant NVA and VC offensive, neither he or anyone in the chain of command anticipated the breadth and magnitude of the attacks that would occur. When they launched the Tet Offensive, the NVA and VC were seeking a decisive victory in a short period of time, a significant change from their prior strategy of protracted warfare designed to wear down the United States and ARVN forces.

The simultaneous surprise attacks during Tet were waged in populated areas, and in particular, places where the United States had a strong military presence. Most notably, these attacks were predominantly executed in the areas of Saigon, in the south, and Hue in the north. Hue is located close to the Vietnamese Demilitarized Zone ("DMZ"), the de-facto border between North and South Vietnam. However, it was Hue's proximity to Highway 1, an important supply line for United States and South Vietnam forces from the coastal city of Da Nang that made Hue a primary target. Saigon, the capital of Vietnam and primary location of the United States military command, was an obvious target as well.

The Battle of Hue began on the morning of January 30 and lasted for 26 days. This battle fought primarily by the United States Marines was one of the longest and bloodiest battles of the Vietnam War. In the years that followed, mass graves were discovered and it became evident that during the four-week attack, a large-scale massacre of men,

3. Infantry Bound

women, children and infants had been carried out by the NVA and VC against anyone sympathetic to the United States forces in the region, and there were also allegations that South Vietnamese "revenge squads" searched out and executed people sympathetic to the NVA and VC.

The battle for Saigon also began on the morning of January 30 with an assault on the six-acre park that housed the Independence Palace and President Thieu's private residence, followed quickly by an assault on the U.S. embassy just three blocks away. Other targets included the Vietnamese Navy Headquarters located on the Saigon River waterfront and on the National Broadcasting Station.

Tan Son Nhut Air Base, located on the northwest outskirts of Saigon, also came under heavy attack, and was quickly overwhelmed. U.S. security personnel were pinned down in their bunkers while hundreds of NVA and VC soldiers were inside the perimeter of the base. NVA and VC troops had already entered the Go Vap Logistical Area outside the base, and had overrun the nearby Phu Hoa Dong Artillery Training Center and the Co Loa Armored Training Center. The most successful attack launched by the NVA and VC was on the U.S. Joint General Staff headquarters located near the base. Simultaneous attacks also occurred all over Saigon's periphery, including attacks on Cholon, the Phu Tho Racetrack, the Long Binh military complex and the Bien Hoa Airbase.

One very important aspect of the Tet Offensive specifically and the Vietnam War generally was that by 1968 most homes in the United States had televisions. These televisions brought witness to the events of one of the most tumultuous years in the history of the United States and of the world. When the NVA and VC attacked the U.S. Embassy in Saigon, and were able to get inside the complex's courtyard, the breach was televised into the living rooms of America, and America was stunned. "While the enemy failed in (the) Republic of Vietnam, he won in the United States" observed Abrams, a United States Army general who was commanding military operations in Vietnam at the time.[5]

After the Tet Offensive nothing really changed at Fort Jackson, although there was definitely more urgency, more tension. I tried not to think about what was going on over there too much; I would be there soon enough. Although many of us volunteered for Airborne Training after Advanced Infantry Training, almost no one got in. The demand for troops on the ground in Vietnam was the priority.

Walter Cronkite, the anchorman for the *CBS Evening News*, traveled to Vietnam and filed several reports from there. I am glad we didn't have much time for television at Fort Jackson. I am glad I didn't hear him say he thought we could never win the war.

February 27, 1968—Commentary by Walter Cronkite

> It seems now more certain than ever that the bloody experience of Vietnam is to end in a stalemate. This summer's almost certain standoff will either end in real give-and-take negotiations or terrible escalation; and for every means we have to escalate, the enemy can match us, and that applies to invasion of the North, the use of nuclear weapons, or the mere commitment of one hundred, or two hundred, or three hundred thousand more American troops to the battle. And with each escalation, the world comes closer to the brink of cosmic disaster.
>
> To say that we are closer to victory today is to believe, in the face of the evidence, the optimists who have been wrong in the past. To suggest we are on the edge of defeat is to yield to unreasonable pessimism. To say that we are mired in stalemate seems the only realistic, yet unsatisfactory, conclusion.
>
> On the off chance that military and political analysts are right, in the next few months we must test the enemy's intentions, in case this is indeed his last big gasp before negotiations. But it is increasingly clear to this reporter that the only rational way out then will be to negotiate, not as victors, but as an honorable people who lived up to their pledge to defend democracy and did the best they could.

When I completed Advanced Infantry Training, I received orders to report to the Army Terminal in Oakland, California, to be deployed to Vietnam. I went home on leave first for about a week. I am not sure going home was a good idea. Although of course I wanted to, and I know my family wanted to see me before I shipped out, no one knew what to say. There wasn't anything good to say about where I was going. I think going home before shipping out was hard on everyone, especially on my parents, and definitely on me.

3. Infantry Bound

I wish I could say that San Francisco was amazing, that seeing the Pacific Ocean for the first time was amazing, that standing on the dock looking across the bay to San Francisco and the Golden Gate Bridge with my cousin Al and his wife Donna was amazing, but I was very preoccupied at the time. I think I was afraid I would never see it again.

March 11, 1968   Letter to Mom and Dad from Al

Dear Doris and George,

I thought I'd drop you a line to let you know that Herb got off all right. It was good to see him again and Donna and I were happy we could meet him and help him out. Sunday morning we ate a big breakfast and then drove around Oakland before dropping him off at the Army terminal. That place is a real mess and very confusing. Anyway, he looks real good and happy. He will be back before you know it. When he writes to you please send us his address so we can drop him a line.

Chapter 4

Hello, Vietnam

The plane made a steep decline into the Ben Hoa Air Force Base near Saigon. It was a commercial TWA plane like the typical planes people used for business or personal travel. In the Nam, they called it the freedom plane because it also takes troops home after their deployment. There wasn't really any chance of ground to air fire but the pilot wasn't taking any chances, not since the Tet Offensive began. When we stepped off the plane the heat was really oppressive and the air was thick. A group of very tan guys in frayed sun-bleached fatigues passed by as we exited the plane. "Good luck FNGs," they yelled to us.

I found out later FNGs were "fucking new guys." But you didn't stay new in Vietnam for very long. They were loading body bags onto a plane nearby. I decided that day on the tarmac that I'd probably never make it home, so I better just accept that and focus on staying alive one day at a time.

March 14, 1968

Dear Mom and Dad,

Well here I am in this beautiful land of dust and jungles. We got in yesterday afternoon at Ben Hoa air force base. Then we took a bus to Long Binh about 6 miles away from where I am right now. We are about 27 miles from Saigon but they say we will only be here for 24 to 72 hours and then will be shipped to our unit.

When we landed it was 90 degrees and it stays pretty hot all night. On the buses we passed through a village, it was really something to see the way the people here live. Some of them were out in the yard taking a bath in a tub of water. The shacks they live in are really run down and they weren't

4. Hello, Vietnam

much to start with so you can imagine what they look like when they are run down.

The camp I am at is a replacement station, when they have formations (three times a day) they call off the names of the guys being shipped out to their units. At the morning formation they give out work details, I was lucky this morning and didn't get one.

We do have a roof to sleep under, and I mean that literally, its just 2 × 4s holding up a roof with screening around it. We have a place where we can take cold showers and shave, we also have a beer hall and a PX. Actually the conditions right now are better than I expected but I am not going to judge Vietnam until I get to my unit.

They say this camp hasn't been hit since January and they have helicopters flying around all the time to check the surrounding area. When we landed at the airport there was a group waiting to take that flight home and I have never seen a group of happy guys like that before.

This camp is all dust and sand and it looks like it hasn't rained here in months. Before we landed we were flying over Vietnam for the first time, I got a little funny feeling in my stomach so I guess I was a bit nervous. I think my year here is going to go by fast.

The jungle fatigues we got are very light and cool and the boots are light also. Part of the boot is made of canvas and they have some type of steel in the sole to prevent punctures so I don't know how they can be lighter than the regular type but they are.

When the sun comes up in the morning it really looks big and it looks like it is very close to me. There is a 14 hour time difference between here and Connecticut.

I will probably ship out tomorrow or the day after. Here is a map of Vietnam. Hold onto it so you can see where I will be at my new unit when I write. I am at Long Binh now.

This map was given to us so we would know where we could go to see a dentist, and on the back, there were instructions on how to keep our teeth healthy while we were there. The idea that we would be able to go see a dentist while we were in Vietnam, or we would be able to keep our teeth healthy ... well that was not the Vietnam I experienced.

The jungle boots I was given when I got to Vietnam were designated by the military as the "M-1966 Jungle Boot." They were part combat boot and part canvas sneaker. The upper part was cotton canvas, the toe and heel were leather, and they had a special type of rubber

Vietnam Stories I Never Told

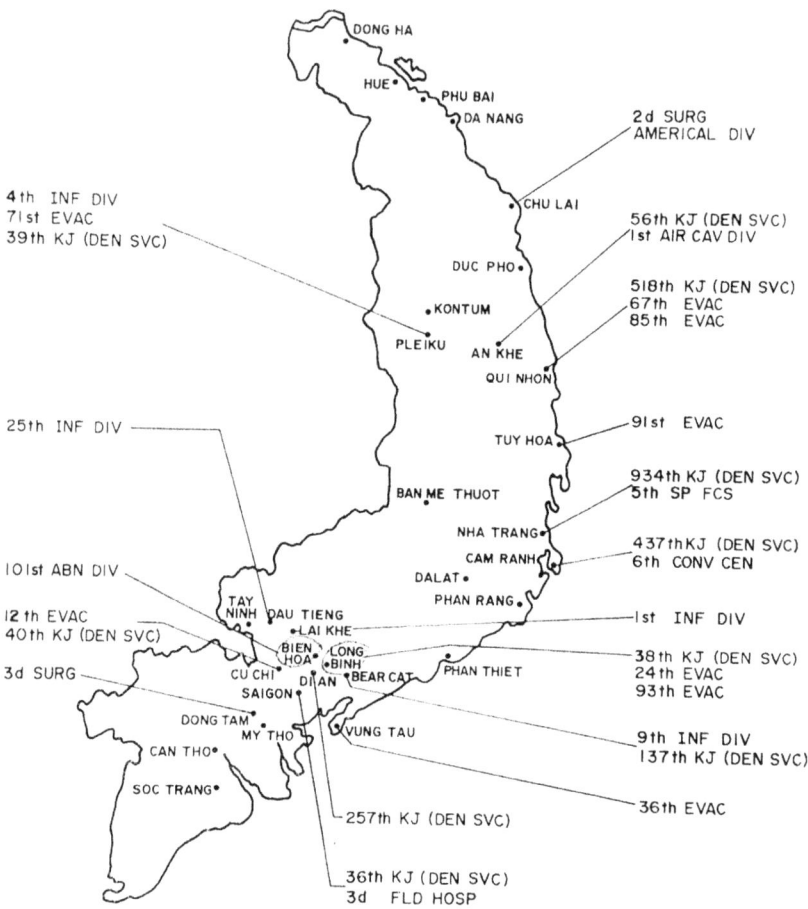

Map given to Jansen when he arrived at Long Bien, sent home with letter dated March 14, 1968. The map identifies location of dental treatment facilities available to military personnel while in-country (South Vietnam).

sole. The boots had eyelets near the bottom of the canvas portion that were intended to allow mud and moisture to drain out and they had a stainless-steel plate to prevent foot injuries. Those eyelets definitely did not allow the kind of mud and moisture we were in to drain out, but I guess the concept was good.

4. Hello, Vietnam

DENTAL CARE IN VIETNAM

There are over 80 dental treatment facilities in South Vietnam dispersed over 50,000 square miles. On the back of this sheet is a map showing where some of these dental treatment facilities are located. In many areas there is more than one clinic and often it is up to the individual to seek out the clinic servicing his unit. DO THIS EARLY IN YOUR TOUR.

Since many of you will spend some time in the field, it is important that you maintain a good, clean mouth to prevent suffering from tooth or gum diseases. DO NOT FORGET YOUR TOOTHBRUSH WHEN YOU LEAVE FOR THE FIELD. There are folding toothbrushs available in the PX, if you desire a compact one.

If you lose your toothbrush, while away from camp, here are some tips that will help you keep your teeth clean:

1. Swish a mouthful of water vigorously around your teeth following each meal. If water is scarce, then swallow it after swishing.

2. Take a small branch, such as a bamboo stick, and shred one end. This bristle-like end can then be rubbed over the teeth.

3. Remove the bark from a small twig and then sharpen this twig to a triangular tip. Use this to gently remove soft debris from the teeth.

4. Wrap a finger inside of your handkerchief, dip it in your water and rub the teeth and gums clean.

Remember, clean teeth feel smooth to the tongue.

!!!!YOU CAN PREVENT DENTAL DISEASES!!!!

Flip side of map given to Jansen when he arrived at Long Bien, sent home with letter dated March 14, 1968. "Dental Care in Vietnam" provides instructions on accessing dental care and proper care of teeth when we are in the field, in-country (South Vietnam).

March 16, 1968

Dear Mom and Dad,

It is Saturday afternoon and we are still at the replacement station. I am in good spirits so far, actually I feel better than I did at Fort Jackson. There are only about 5 of us left out of my group that haven't been shipped out to our units so I figure I will be shipping out soon. I must be getting used to being away from home because I remember when I first went to South Carolina I felt like I was going a million miles away from home and I was really feeling bad, but when I came here I didn't feel that way. When I was at Fort Jackson all I could think about was getting home but now I know that it's so far away so I haven't thought about it too much. Don't get me wrong I'd rather be there than here but I guess I am just learning to live with it.

I can't say that I am getting used to the heat but I am getting used to being hot and sweaty all the time. I have been taking salt tablets and they help a lot. I hope it wasn't the malaria tablet that gave me the runs Monday because I found out we are supposed to take one every week. One thing the army has taught me, that's to appreciate civilian life. When I was home even running an errand for someone was a pleasure so you can imagine how much I enjoyed myself when I went some place, when I get out of the army I am going to be the happiest guy alive for the rest of my life.

For some reason I never seem to get hungry, I eat my meals but I never get hungry before the meals like I did in the states, I guess it's because of the heat.

We have a paper called the Stars and Stripes *over here with the news of the war and major news from the states.*

I really hope you're not sitting around worrying about me. I guess if I were in your position I would worry but please try not to. Say hello to the family for me; you can tell grandma that I am still alive and kicking so her prayers must be doing me good.

P.S. I really go for this free mail.

March 18, 1968

Dear Mom and Dad,

Sunday afternoon I was shipped out of the replacement station, guess where they took me? To another replacement station only this time it is for the 25th Division. Well today I got my orders, my mailing address will be Co A 4th Bn, 9th Inf. I will be staying here for 4 more days for some more training. Right now I am in Cu Chi, if you look at the map you'll see it, it's not far from Saigon. The company I am going to is on the Cambodian border and the base camp is at Tay Ninh which is also on the map.

On the way here we rode on trucks from Long Bien, I wish I had my camera out because I couldn't begin to tell you all the things I saw and they say a picture is worth a thousand words well I could have used the whole film. We passed through Saigon, you should see the traffic there, there are people on bikes, trucks, and a few cars going in all different directions and the army

4. Hello, Vietnam

truck drivers drive right over them if they don't move. I have a lot more to say but I feel like I haven't slept in a week so I think I will catch up on it tonight.

Saigon is situated in southeast Vietnam and was built around the Saigon River, approximately 1,000 miles from Hanoi (the capital of North Vietnam). The city is located close to the Mekong Delta where the Mekong River spills into the South China Sea. The average elevation is just five meters above sea level, and as a result Saigon is surrounded by tidal flats. These tidal flats were modified by the French during the French colonial period in the mid–nineteenth century into a maze of canals that allow rice crops to be grown three times each year. Saigon is also just 12 miles from the Cambodian border to the west.

In the seventeenth and eighteenth centuries Vietnam was divided between the north and south by the Song-Gianh River. The north was called Tonkin and was ruled by the House of Trinh. The south was called Dang Trong, which means "Inner Realm" and was ruled by the Nguyen Clan. The 17th parallel located at the Ben Hai River in the Quang Tri Province, which divided Vietnam into North Vietnam and South Vietnam beginning in 1954, is located just south of this prior historically significant dividing line. South Vietnam was renamed Cochinchina in 1862 and Saigon was the capital of Cochinchina from 1862 to 1954.

During this period Saigon became a major port city. Cochinchina's primary export product was rice grown in the Mekong Delta. The wealth generated by export was evidenced by the beautiful villas built along paved, wide tree-lined boulevards, and ornate public buildings and railway lines running north and south of the city. Architecturally magnificent buildings like the Central Post Office, built by French architect Vildieu, the Opera House, the Hotel de Ville and the Notre Dame Cathedral were built.

Although Cochinchina was occupied by the Japanese from 1940 to 1945, it continued to operate under French colonial authority. When the Japanese surrendered, ending World War II in August of 1945, the communist front Viet Minh,[1] led by Ho Chi Minh, declared independence from France and established the Democratic Republic of Vietnam (DRV) with a provisional ruling government in Saigon. However, the French, aided by the British and even some Japanese troops forced the Viet Minh out of Saigon.

In 1946, even though Ho Chi Minh had accepted France's offer to allow Vietnam to be an autonomous state within the French Union rather than to continue on as a French Protectorate, resistance by the Viet Minh erupted almost immediately around Saigon and marked the beginning of the First Indochina War between France and the Viet Minh.

During the first few years of the war the Viet Minh lacked the weapons and training to successfully oust the French. Later, under the leadership of Vo Nguyen Giap, the Viet Minh were trained in guerrilla warfare and adapted ideas and techniques from a pamphlet written by Chinese communist leader Mao Zedong on how to win a revolutionary war. They withdrew to the mountains in the north and immersed themselves in local villages there. This allowed the Viet Minh to build up political support among the villagers and by moving with and among these villagers they also had cover for their guerrilla warfare activities. As a result, support for the Viet Minh grew strongest in the north, the Viet Minh's area of operation and the location of their primary base near Hanoi.

In 1949, France established the State of South Vietnam with an alternative government lead by Bao Dai where there was more wealth (due to rice exportation) and more religious diversity.[2] While the population of South Vietnam generally favored independence from France they were leery of communism, so Bao Dai's government created the Vietnamese National Army to fight alongside the French against the Viet Minh in the north. At this point the First Indochina War took on traditional characteristics of war, two armies fighting each other, both equipped with modern weapons. The weapons used by the Vietnamese National Army and the French army were supplied by the United States. The weapons used by the Viet Minh were supplied by newly communist China and the Soviet Union.

In July 1954, following a decisive defeat of the French in the Battle

4. Hello, Vietnam

of Dien Bien Phu, a Geneva conference (the Geneva Accords) ended the First Indochina war. France agreed to permanently withdraw from Vietnam, and Vietnam was partitioned into northern and southern zones, separated by the Ben Hai River at the 17th parallel. Still under the leadership of Ho Chi Minh, the Viet Minh were given complete control of the northern half of the country which retained the name DRV. The southern half of the country gained complete independence from France and retained the name of the State of South Vietnam under the leadership of Bao Dai.

Three military agreements and six unilateral declarations made up the "Final Declaration of the Geneva Conference (July 21, 1954)." The Geneva Accords was negotiated by and between representatives of the newly socialist France, Cambodia, China, Laos, United Kingdom, Soviet Union, United States, the Viet Minh (DRV) and the State of South Vietnam. Even though the United States and the State of South Vietnam had been party to the negotiations, both made clear they did not agree to be bound by its terms.

This Geneva Accords was only meant to be in force pending elections to be held in July 1956 to reunify the country, and allowed for the free movement of people between North and South Vietnam for 300 days before the border would be sealed. This was called "Operation Passage to Freedom" by the U.S. Navy and during this period the U.S. Navy and ships assigned to the Military Sealift Transportation Service transported 310,000 people, including civilians and soldiers from DRV to the State of South Vietnam.[3] Approximately 14,000 civilians relocated in the opposite direction, from the State of South Vietnam to DVR, during that time. The civilians that migrated north were believed to be Viet Minh (southern communists).

In 1955 Bao Dai was ousted as premier of the State of Vietnam in a referendum by his prime minister, Ngo Dinh Diem. Diem had the support of the United States and when Diem took control of the State of South Vietnam, he renamed it "The Republic of Vietnam," with Saigon as its capital. In July 1955 Diem announced that the Republic of Vietnam would not participate in the elections to reunify the country, citing the fact that the Republic of Vietnam (then the State of South

Vietnam) had not signed the Geneva Accords and was therefore, not bound by it.

During the (Ngo Dinh) Diem regime, from 1955 to 1963, Saigon was the center of the Republic of South Vietnam's economic activity. During that period the United States provided nearly $2 billion in aid to promote democracy and capitalism, and the country grew rapidly. Even so, South Vietnam remained very dependent on aid from the United States and on imports from other countries.

Diem reportedly clashed with U.S. advisors and had a different understanding of Democracy and of Catholicism, which Diem practiced. Buddhism is followed by many of the Vietnamese, alongside Confucianism, Vietnamese folk tradition and the teachings of Tao. Diem was accused of favoring Catholics and persecuting Buddhists. Diem's brother, Ngo Dinh Nhu, who served in Diem's government is believed to be responsible for the violent suppression of a Buddhist protest demonstration in Hue on May 8, 1963, leading to a "Buddhist Crisis."

In June 1963 a Buddhist monk, Thich Quang Duc, burned himself alive in protest of the Diem regime, and photographs of the scene were seen around the world. There are disagreements over whether the Diem regime did suppress Buddhism in the manner described by journalists who were there on the ground in South Vietnam. Many of the sensational reports published in *The New York Times* at the time regarding the purported suppression of Buddhists by the Diem regime later proved to be exaggerated.

At the time, Diem believed that many of the participants in the Buddhist movement that lead to the Buddhist crisis were Viet Minh infiltrators intent on destabilizing his government and overthrowing his regime. In 1960 an organization called the National Liberation Front of South Vietnam (NLF) whose sole objective was to topple the Diem government and reunify North and South Vietnam had been established. Many of its core members were Viet Minh who had relocated to the North during the Operation Passage to Freedom and had been retrained in guerrilla warfare. They became known as the Viet Cong. Diem believed they had been sent back south by Hanoi, via the

4. Hello, Vietnam

Ho Chi Minh Trail, to instigate unrest. Diem's belief that the Viet Cong were responsible for the Buddhist uprising was corroborated by many other accounts at the time. Nevertheless, the accusations of suppression of Buddhism further damaged Diem's relationship with the United States and even his relationship with his own generals.

On August 7, 1963, Diem met with Marguerite Higgins, a reporter for *The Herald Tribune* and former bureau chief in Berlin and Tokyo, who had been asked to go to Vietnam to meet with Diem and report back. Before departing, Higgins met with Lt. Gen. Victor H. Krulak (U.S.M.C, special assistant for counterinsurgency and special activities, Organization of the Joint Chiefs of Staff from 1962 to 1964). Higgins reports that Gen. Krulak told her before she left for Vietnam that the Buddhist agitation in Vietnam was not religious, it was political.[4]

Ms. Higgins interview with Diem lasted for over five hours, and one specific Diem quote she provides seems consistent with the Vietnam I experienced:

> The west must give us a little time. Even though you Westerners do not recognize it in its Oriental form, the spirit of democracy has always been a key part of the best of Asian thought. It is related to all our Asian religions. Indian philosophy conceives of the transcendence of the human soul. Buddha preached the equality of all men. There is the freedom intertwined in the spontaneous emergence of the Taoist being [sic]; and there are the cosmic as well as highly individual virtues of Confucian Jen [Jen meaning the great, or complete, man]. This spiritual basis of democracy is to be found everywhere in Vietnam, especially in our villages, and we are building democracy there. The villages largely run themselves. Gradually, when the war ends, we can move to greater democracy on a national level, drawing from the permanent values of western culture. But it is impossible—a delusion—to think that a solution for Asia consists of blindly copying western methods.[5]

A Congressional delegation led by Rep. Clement J. Zablocki conducted a special study mission to Southeast Asia (Laos, Malaysia, and Vietnam) from October 3 to 19, 1963. While several members of the delegation left with "a preconception that the Diem regime must be liquidated,"[6] upon their return, Rep. Zablocki reported to Gen.

Kurlak on October 28, 1963, that all eight members agreed on the following:

a. Diem, with all his faults, his autocracy, his tolerance of venality and brutality, is durable, and has been winning.
b. There is no visible substitute for Diem—at least none which guarantees improvement; thus actions by U.S. representatives to join with coup plotters, as apparently was true in August, is harmful.
c. The conduct of the resident U.S. press is a grave reflection upon their entire profession. They are arrogant, emotional, unobjective and ill-informed. The case against them is best expressed by their having been repudiated by much of the responsible press.[7]

On November 1, 1963, Diem was assassinated in Saigon in a successful coup d'état by one of his generals, Duong Van Minh. By all accounts the United States was complicit in both the instigation and execution of the coup. Cable 243 "Telegram from the Department of State to the Embassy in Vietnam" was sent on August 24, 1963, to Ambassador Lodge who was at the Embassy in Vietnam at the time. Lodge was believed by some to be strongly anti–Diem, and his interpretation and communication of the contents of the cable to Gen. Duong Van Minh reportedly lead the general to believe that the financial aid provided by the United States to South Vietnam would only continue if Diem was removed from office. Notably, Ambassador Lodge did not share the contents of the telegram with Diem when he met with him on August 26, 1963.[8]

Cable 243 has been described as the "single most controversial cable of the Vietnam War."[9] Gen. Van Minh and Diem's other generals tried to organize a coup d'état to remove Diem from power following the receipt of Cable 243 in late August 1963 but the coup failed to materialize. Soon after the United States began withholding financial aid, and Diem's generals then believed that Diem had to be removed from office to satisfy the United States in order for financial aid from the United States to be restored.[10]

4. Hello, Vietnam

Ms. Higgins quotes Edward R. Murrow as saying: "President Kennedy was very badly served on the issue of Vietnam. Feelings ran so high between the Diem-must go school and the Diem-must-stay school that the processes of reason could not function."[11]

In reaction to the coup and assassination of Diem, Ho Chi Minh is reported to have said "I can scarcely believe the Americans would be so stupid"[12] and the North Vietnamese Politburo issued the following statement:

> The consequences of the 1 November coup d'etat will be contrary to the calculations of the U.S. imperialists.... Diem was one of the strongest individuals resisting the people and Communism. Everything that could be done in the attempt to crush the revolution was carried out by Diem. Diem was one of the most competent lackeys of the US imperialists.... Among the anti–Communists in South Vietnam or exiled in other countries, no one has sufficient political assets and abilities to cause others to obey. Therefore, the lackey administration cannot be stabilized. The coup d'etat on 1 November 1963 will not be the last.[13]

When Gen. Krulak was asked about viability of the new government to be led by Gen. Duong Van Minh during a National Security Council meeting held shortly after the coup, he responded "fifty-fifty." Gen. Van Minh was defeated just a few months later by Gen. Nguyen Khanh, followed by another, and another.

For whatever his strengths and weaknesses, Diem had seemingly created stability for an independent South Vietnam, and following his assassination, South Vietnam as an independent country was never stable again.

On August 2, 1964, the United Sates was conducting covert activities by ship in the Gulf of Tonkin, close to the territorial waters of North Vietnam. Ho Chi Minh's Viet Minh Army responded by attacking the ship. The United States claimed a subsequent attack on a U.S. ship in the Gulf occurred two days later, on August 4, 1964. The claim regarding the second attack later proved to be false,[14] but not before President Johnson asked Congress for broad war powers, and in March 1965 the United States sent the first combat troops to Vietnam to fight alongside the ARVN.

"Good-bye, my darling, hello, Vietnam."[15]

Chapter 5

My M-16 Rifle

Once there were boots on the ground, Saigon was headquarters for United States and South Vietnam's military operations and was still their headquarters when I arrived in Vietnam.

March 25, 1968

Dear Mom and Dad,

I finished my training at Cu Chi yesterday and was flown on a military transport plane to Tay Ninh. I say that I have flown a lot but after I was on that plane a few minutes I knew that I didn't know what flying was until then. We sat on a bench on the side of the wall it was a propeller plane and it didn't have any insulation for the sound and the whole plane shook and vibrated the whole way most of the guys were almost sick after 20 minutes we were in the air.

While I was at Cu Chi I received an M16 rifle and I didn't care for the one I got. It jammed up a lot, it would fire off the first round all right and it wouldn't extract the empty shell so the next round couldn't slide into the chamber with the empty shell in the way and the rifle would jam. To correct it I had to pull out the magazine and pull back the bolt to get the shell out. So with all that to go through I was a little worried.

Well anyway when I got here to my company my squad leader asked me if I would rather carry an M79 grenade launcher and I jumped at the chance. The M79 is about 2½ feet long and weighs about 8 pounds, so it is small and light. It fires a grenade that looks like a large bullet, about 1½ inch wide and 3 inches long, it will fire as far as 450 yards accurately and will kill anybody within 6 yards of where the round lands and would wound anyone within 15 yards, so you see it is quite a weapon. They also fire something similar to a shotgun cartridge; it is called a canister round and has about 4 times as many pellets as a 12-gauge shotgun cartridge. In a few days I will be getting a .45-caliber pistol, everybody who has anything other than an M16 rifle can have a pistol and a holster that hooks on my web belt so I think I will be well armed.

5. My M-16 Rifle

I was pretty lucky to get to the company now because they just came back from being out 42 days and the next 6 days we are just patrolling around the camp and village. Most of the guys are all right and have helped me out. All the guys are complaining that their rifles always jam too so I am really glad that I got the M79. I must say that carrying 50 grenades is a little heavy but I will get used to it. We put in $8 a month and once a day they bring us a cold beer and cold soda when they bring our supplies even if it is by helicopter, its really good when you have been out all day in 110-degree temperatures to get something cold to drink.

When we are on patrol near the village the kids come around trying to sell us sodas, they know the guys want a cold drink so they charge 30 cents for a soda. I won't buy one for that price and if everybody did that they would lower the price but the guys don't care so the prices will stay high. They say that wherever U.S. troops are prices go up because the guys are willing to pay high.

They say we will get at least one hot meal a day when we are in the field (that is when you are outside of the base camp we say the field). There aren't any days off over here and sometimes things are hard but for some crazy reasons I like it better than duty in the states. I miss home but not to the point I used too but I think that is because I have set it in my mind that I won't be going home for a year so I don't think about going home too much. If I thought about it too much it would drive me crazy thinking about how soft and easy I had it when I was a civilian. To sit in one of our living room chairs or sleep in a real bed would really be a luxury to me now.

I think this year is going to do me a lot of good to clear my mind about what I want to do with my life. I had so many girls on my mind before I came here that sometimes I wasn't sure if I was coming or going, that may sound strange for me to say when I am engaged to Sherri but that's the way it was. Maybe when I leave here I will be settled down enough to get married and if I am she will the perfect girl but as it stands I know that I am not ready, I enjoy meeting new girls too much, so I hope this year I can make a decision.

I would like you to send me a few things that I need and can't get to a px to get ... a shaving brush, some pipe cleaners and a brush which is about 9 inches long with twisted wire as a core and hard bristles on or about 3 inches of the end. I think I have seen one in the house it looks like this.

These are to clean my weapon with. Write all the latest gossip and say hello to everybody for me. I hope grandma is doing okay.

Vietnam Stories I Never Told

Drawing in Jansen's letter home dated March 25, 1968, to illustrate the tool he asked his parents to send him that he wanted to use to clean his weapon.

On October 19, 1967, the Committee on Armed Services, House of Representatives, 90th Congress held their first session of the Special Subcommittee on the M-16 Assault Rifle Program.[1] The purpose of the session was to review and discuss the report prepared by Richard Ichord, chairman of the Special Subcommittee on the M-16 Assault Rifle Program. The Special Subcommittee was established on May 3, 1967. The investigation followed reports that dead U.S. soldiers were found next to jammed M-16s they were trying to fix.[2]

In 1958 the Armalite AR-15 high velocity assault rifle ("AR-15"), the precursor to the M-16, was introduced to and tested by the U.S. Army. The AR-15 was a light-weight high velocity rifle that shot a .223 caliper cartridge. The U.S. army had reservations about the suitability of a .223 caliper cartridge for use in combat and rejected the AR-15 for use in combat for that reason. The U.S. Army had, since the year 1903, consistently required any rifle or small arm used in combat to fire a .30 caliber cartridge. The .30 caliber cartridge was considered by the Army to be the optimum size for use in combat.[3]

In late 1958 the U.S. Army conducted an experiment to compare the M-14 using the .30 caliper cartridges, the AR-15 using the .223 caliper cartridge and the Winchester lightweight high velocity military rifle using a .224 caliper cartridge. The experiment was conducted from December 1958 to March 1959. The conclusion reached from the experiment was that a smaller five to seven squad team armed with

5. My M-16 Rifle

a lightweight high velocity weapon would have a better hit distribution and greater hit capacity than an 11 squad team armed with M-14s. The report recommended that a light-weight high velocity assault rifle be developed that had the accuracy characteristics of the Winchester assault rifle and the reliability characteristics of the AR-15 that did not exceed the weapon weight of either. Nevertheless, the Army kept the M-14 in production.[4]

The Air Force continued to test and evaluate the AR-15 and in January 1962 the AR-15 was classified as the standard weapon for the U.S. Air Force inventory. The Air Force was advised to use the .223 caliper 55 grain metal jacket bullet manufactured by Remington Arms, Inc., that was developed in cooperation with Armalite for use in the AR-15. The bullet weighed half as much as the .30 caliber bullet and traveled a flatter trajectory giving it less vertical error. As advised, the U.S. Air Force awarded the contract to produce the AR-15s to Armalite and the contract produce the .223 caliper bullet to Remington.[5]

The secretary of defense approved the procurement of a small batch of AR-15s, ammunition and spare parts to be provided to the ARVN for evaluation. The Vietnamese unit commanders and U.S. advisors who participated in the evaluation all agreed that the AR-15 was the more desirable weapon for use in Vietnam. However, when a substantial order was subsequently placed to equip certain ARVN troops with the AR-15 weapons and ammunition, the commander in chief of the Pacific Forces, Admiral Harry D. Felt objected due to the cost and the effort that would be required to implement and train the ARVN troops for the weapon's use.[6]

In September 1962, a report was submitted by the Office of the Controller to the secretary of defense comparing the cost effectiveness of the M-14 to the AR-15 since the AR-15 assault rifle was already being used by the Air Force. The report concluded that the AR-15 was the superior weapon. Secretary McNamara, the secretary of defense, contacted the secretary of the army requesting the view of the Department of the Army regarding this report. In response, the secretary of the army ordered an "impartial and objective evaluation of the relative effectiveness of the three weapons" (the M-14, AR-15 and a Soviet rifle, the AK-47).[7] This impartial and objective evaluation concluded that the M-14 was acceptable for use by the U.S. Army and the AR-15, although lighter than the M-14, was not considered a suitable replacement for a list of stated reasons, including that its adoption would violate NATO standardization agreements. Of relevance here is that the NATO standardization agreements referred to were in fact agreements that the United States Army had itself forced upon NATO.[8]

The secretary of the army apparently felt there were reasons to question the objectivity of the Army's conclusions. In December 1962, the Secretary directed the Department of the Army Inspector General to investigate the circumstances surrounding the Army's "impartial and objective evaluation." The Inspector General report indicated bias or prejudice against the AR-15 in favor of the M-14, most notably because the reporting of test results were mixed with personal observation, the tone and verbiage of the findings tended to favor the M-14, and the attitudes of certain personnel involved in the evaluation were favorable toward the M-14 "to the degree that these attitudes may have caused subjective treatment of test results in analysis and reporting."[9]

Following the Inspector General's report, the U.S. Army procured 85,000 AR-15 assault rifles. An Army memorandum dated April 1963 described the procurement procedures and also indicated that certain changes to the AR-15 design were required. These included the addition of a manual bolt closure device, the redesign of magazine, and modification of the chamber throat to assist in the extraction of the entire cartridge upon clearing the weapon.[10]

This final problem that needed to be fixed, modification of the chamber throat to assist in the extraction of the entire cartridge upon clearing the weapon, was caused by the dimensional incompatibility of the ammunition within the rifle chamber. This incompatibility was due to the Army's decision to use a kind of ammunition different from the ammunition the weapon was designed to use.

The AR-15 was developed, tested, and evaluated using commercial ammunition loaded with a single-base tubular grain[11] that had a coating to control the rate of burn (the .223 caliper 55 grain metal jacket bullet). Between the time the M-16 was authorized and the time

5. My M-16 Rifle

it was produced, the composition of the propellant in the ammunition was changed to double-base ball propellant.[12,13]

Although the secretary of defense had ordered that any modifications made to the AR-15 should only be made by request to the weapons manufacturer and in consultation with the weapons designer, according to testimony this order was not followed. Most notably, the weapons designer did not support the changes the Army proposed for the manual bolt closure device and for the change in the ammunition. Nevertheless, the requested modifications were made, with the resulting weapon designated as the M-16.[14]

After reports of malfunctions of the M-16, the Army Weapons Command indicated that the major reason for the malfunction was not in the design but rather was due to the troops not adequately cleaning their weapons. Efforts were made to improve instruction on cleaning and distribution of cleaning materials. However, the real culprit was soon identified ... the ammunition.

A study in November 1965 indicated that most malfunctions of the M-16 were related to an interaction of ammunition (and belt link) deficiencies including weapon fouling, cycling of weapons in excess of design rates, and misfires. Fouling, caused by the ball propellant, resulted from rapid carbon buildup and caused most of the failures to extract. The cycling of weapons in excess of design rates occurred because the ball propellant cycles weapons faster than the original .223 single base tubular grain propellant, resulting in failure of the bolt to remain to the rear after the last round is fired from the magazine, failure to eject, and magazine feeding problems. The problems using the ball propellant were identified by several parties at several junctures beginning in 1964.[15]

The Army's response to this problem was not to go back to using the original propellant, but rather to design a heavier buffer for the weapon to slow down the cycle rate. The buffer modification was approved in January 1966 but not incorporated into the rifle production until December 1966, eleven months later.[16]

In summary, the Congressional panel convened in May 1967 concluded that the major contributor to the malfunction of the M-16 in

Vietnam Stories I Never Told

Vietnam resulted from the use of ammunition loaded with ball propellant. The change to ball propellant was not justified or supported by tests. The sole source provider of ball propellant had a long-term close relationship with the Army and that may have influenced the decision makers to change the propellant to the ball propellant. Most of the modifications to the M-16 were made to address the issues caused by the ball propellant ammunition and were only necessary because of it. The officials at the Department of the Army were aware of the adverse effect of the ball propellant as early as March 1964. The Congressional panel concluded the failure of the officials with authority in the Army to take corrective action bordered on criminal negligence.[17]

In early 1967 production of a modified M-16, designated the M-16A1, began. The M-16A1 included several improvements including a bolt assist, chrome-plated bore, a hatch door opening in the butt to store a cleaning kit and several other minor modifications. Although the U.S. military adopted and began distributing the new M-16A1s in 1967, when I got to Vietnam most of the guys in my company still had the old M-16s.

I wonder how many guys were in the mess of their lives and died or were wounded because their M-16 jammed, or because the other guys in their squad couldn't give them cover to pull back, because their M-16s were jammed.

Chapter 6

The Manchus

The official designation of my company is the 25th Infantry Division, Fourth Battalion of the Ninth Infantry Regiment, Alpha Company. The 25th Infantry Division was known as "Tropic Lightning" because of the lightning bolt on the Division patch. The Fourth Battalion of the Ninth Infantry Regiment are known as the "Manchus." There were four companies in the "Manchu" Battalion: Alpha, Bravo, Charlie, and Delta companies.

From a structural standpoint, a company is part of a battalion, a battalion is part of a regiment, and a regiment is part of a division. From an operational or strategic standpoint, a battalion is part of a brigade. Brigades have a stated purpose or objective, and usually a brigade is made up of battalions from different regiments, and often battalions or the equivalent are from the other branches of service (Air Force, Marine Corps and/or Navy).

In Vietnam the United States military was divided into four Corps Tactical Zones. These were also called military regions. The most critical of the four Corps Tactical Zones was the Special Capital Zone, Corps III which included Saigon. Each Corps was an organizational concept, centralizing the administration and command of each particular region.

Located closest to North Vietnam is I–Corp. The demilitarized zone (DMZ) was the I–Corps' northernmost boundary. I–Corps borders Laos to the west and the South China Sea to the east. II-Corps is in the central highlands of Vietnam, bordering I–Corps to the north, both Laos and Cambodia to the west and the South China Sea to the east. II-Corps covers the greatest physical area. III-Corps is a densely populated and fertile terrain, bordering II-Corps to the north, Cambodia to the west, and the China Sea to the east. Although III-Corps covers a relatively small physical area, III-Corps includes the Capital Special Zone, Saigon. IV-Corps is the marshy Mekong delta bordering III-Corps to the north, Cambodia to the west and the South China Sea to the east. IV-Corps includes the entire of Mekong Delta, where the Mekong River empties into the South China Sea. IV-Corps is the rice bowl of Vietnam and before the war, one of the largest exporters of rice in the world.

The Twenty-fifth Infantry division that I was assigned to was operating in III-Corps. Lt. Gen. Frederick C. Weyland was in command of III-Corps at the time and he was responsible for 33 U.S. Army combat maneuver battalions and six Free World forces combat maneuver battalions organized in ten military bases that circled Saigon. The bases were located close enough to defend Saigon but far enough away to have proximity to the enemy bases and enemy units located further into the countryside between Saigon and Cambodia where the search and destroy missions were being carried out.

I was assigned to Alpha Company along with Wagner, another FNG. There were four platoons in Alpha Company, one mortar platoon and three rifle platoons. Each platoon had three or four squads. Wagner and I were assigned to the third platoon (a rifle platoon), first squad. Saylor was in our squad. He had been in-country for a few months.

The squad leader was Sgt. Davis. From the very beginning Wagner and I knew we were lucky. Davis was one of the most reassuring people I have ever met. We all felt safe with him, even when we were in great danger. Davis, Wagner, Saylor and I became best friends, maybe the best friends I have ever had.

Davis was from West Virginia. He grew up in a small rural town there and joined the Army after high school. He deployed to Germany and spent a year there before his assignment in Vietnam. Davis arrived in Vietnam as a sergeant, and he became a squad leader. Although he arrived only a few months before Wagner and me, he was already experienced. He was in-country during Tet.

6. *The Manchus*

Since Davis enlisted, he was classified "Regular Army." Guys that enlisted had "RA" before their service numbers and guys that were drafted had "U.S." before their service number. Enlistees were obligated to serve for three years while draftees were only obligated to serve for two years. I was U.S. even though I had asked to be drafted early. The whole RA versus U.S. thing was only brought up in basic training where you have to identify yourself as RA or U.S., the implication being that RAs were more than the "Regular Army," they were the "Real Army."

Most RAs were not in the infantry. RAs were able to select a Military Occupation Specialty (MOS) and most RAs selected something other than the infantry. For some reason Davis selected infantry.

Wagner was from a coal-mining town in Kentucky. He is married and talked about his wife all the time. He was drafted, so he didn't have any choice about shipping out, and I think the timing was really difficult for him. He and wife had married not long before he was drafted and they were still getting used to married life. Whenever there was a lull in letters from his wife it just about drove him crazy.

Saylor was from Alabama. He was in-country during Tet also. He was so unassuming you would think he had just arrived. Some guys treated the FNGs like FNGs. Not Saylor. Right away the four of us, Davis, Saylor, Wagner, and I were a team, and we stayed that way.

A few weeks before we got to Tay Ninh Base Camp the Manchus were ambushed on patrol near Hoc Mon, outside of Saigon. There was a fire support base at Hoc Mon.[1] The objective of the troops patrolling outside the fire support base is to support and defend the fire support base and look for the enemy.

On March 1, 1968, the Manchus were conducting sweeps of the area surrounding the base to make sure the area was clear.[2] Late in the day they set up in night defensive positions around the perimeter around the base. From these night defensive positions each company sent out one of their rifle platoons for night ambush patrols.

During the night, after the area had been secured, and just a few hundred yards from the Manchu's night defensive positions, more than 200 enemy troops had move into concealed positions. Army intelligence indicated their presence, and the Manchus were sent out to find them.

Alpha and Bravo companies were ordered to secure Bridge 11 on Highway 248, located near AP Nam Thanh, close to where they had established their defensive position the night before. Alpha Company secured one side of the bridge, and Bravo Company secured the other, using a military strategy called "out posting."

To secure the bridge, each company formed a column on each side of the bridge, then started moving forward. Once the lead position of each column moved a short distance into an unsecured area, the lead position would step off the line and moved several meters to the side and take up a defensive position. Then the column would continue to move forward, and the new lead position would step off the line and do the same thing. This would continue until the whole company was off the roadway, providing security for whomever followed.

Charlie Company and Delta Company were ordered to move south over the Bridge 11, passing through Alpha Company and Bravo Company's defensive positions on each side, and continue south to Bridge 12. Alpha Company was ordered to fall in behind Delta Company, and Bravo Company was held in reserve.

The next section of the highway, between Bridge 11 and Bridge 12, had not been secured that morning. Although the area had been secured the night before, it should have been secured again before troops moved through. Charlie Company had been late joining Delta Company by Bridge 11, so they moved quickly to get back on schedule and didn't take the time to secure the roadway ahead of them. They moved more than 500 meters along the roadway toward Bridge 12 without realizing the danger they were in.

As Charlie Company moved toward Bridge 12 they were ambushed. Delta Company came under fire as they tried to help Charlie Company. Alpha Company and Bravo Company, still in their defensive positions along Bridge 11, were under small arms fire and were

6. The Manchus

pinned down. By noon that day, 48 of the 92 men in Charlie Company were dead, and 29 were wounded.

By the end of the day, the Battalion CO was relieved of his command. The rest of the battalion was ordered back to the First Brigade's main base camp in Tay Ninh. They had been out in the field for 42 days.

> *New York Times,* Monday, March 4, 1968: *"48 U.S. Soldiers Killed in Ambush on Edge of Saigon" (in part)*
>
> SAIGON, South Vietnam. March 4 (Monday)—Forty-eight Americans have been killed and 28 wounded in an ambush of a United States infantry company four miles north of Tan Son Nhut Air Base in Saigon. Twenty enemy soldiers were killed. Fewer than half of the company's 150 soldiers escaped unscathed, a United States Military spokesman reported yesterday.
>
> The ambush, one of the worst in the war, occurred Saturday (March 2nd). Most of the American casualties came in an 8-minute burst of fire from machine guns, automatic rifle, mortars and rocket launchers. Mines were also detonated.
>
> The ambush near Saigon occurred about 9:20 A.M. when troops of the United States 25th Infantry Division marched through an old French rubber plantation. They took the road that runs between parallel canals several years apart.
>
> Well-informed military official say that the enemy unit—probably a reinforced company of perhaps 150 men—had hidden along the banks of these canals. In front of the advancing Americans another canal cut across the roads, but it was spanned by a bridge. *"Apparently when the lead elements of the company got to the bridge everything cut loose."* The official said. *"Then the VC broke contact and that was it. It was all over in about 8 minutes."* All of the units' officers—ordinarily there are six in a company—were either killed or wounded.

Even before the ambush the Manchus had lost many men and needed replacements. Wagner and I were two of the replacements.

Chapter 7

Saddle Up

The first thing they did when we arrived at the base camp in Tay Ninh was give us all this stuff to put on. "OK, saddle up!"

They called it saddle up, meaning put on all your gear and get ready to move. The standard issue in terms of gear included a uniform, made up of lightweight fatigues, underwear, socks and boots, a weapon and ammunition, hand grenades (both fragmentation and smoke grenades), a canteen or canteens, an entrenchment tool (shovel), a supply of empty sandbags, a machete, a gas mask and a helmet with liner, a poncho and liner, a claymore mine and a flak jacket. Also issued was a web belt (various items connected to the web belt like canteens, entrenchment tool, and gas mask, etc.) as well as a rucksack or alternatively a knapsack and several days' supply of C rations. This could add up to eighty pounds or more dry and if the poncho liner got wet, even more.

I felt like the stuff I was carrying weighed more than I did. Then this guy Garner walked over to Wagner and starts grabbing some of the gear, throwing it on the ground. "Take all that shit off. You aren't going use this, or this, or this, or this...." Wagner was standing right next to me, so I started taking off all that stuff as well, throwing it on the ground next to his. "If you carry this shit around all day, you will be dead before you even see a single NVA," Garner was saying as he started down the line. We were pretty confused, but we hadn't seen anything yet. I already had most of that stuff off when he got to me.

The guys that gave us all the stuff to wear aren't the guys who actually go out into the field. They stay at the base camp and they

7. Saddle Up

have all these books that tell them what we need in the field, but since they've never been in the field, they have no idea what it is like or what we really need or maybe they were just following protocol. Garner was the platoon sergeant and had seen plenty of action, so he knew.

While many of these items were needed at times, they were not all needed every day. We typically did not wear flak jackets. Flak jackets did nothing to stop bullets and with the front open, as they were typically worn, they had limited utility stopping shrapnel. We did not regularly carry the entrenchment tool or claymore mines. When we needed them, a supply would usually be choppered out to us. There were times, though, when we moved every day, that we did hump both.

One thing Garner told us to take off was a gas mask. I wished later that I had kept mine because they started gassing us in April. I don't mean the NVA or VC, I mean our guys gassed us. We heard they started using gas right after Tet, so maybe Garner wasn't used to needing a gas mask, but I found a gas mask is really something you need if you are out in the field.

During our first few weeks at Tay Ninh base camp, we did day patrols and I got used to what it was like being out on patrol, and I got used to getting eaten by red ants. Our platoon was mostly made up of southern Whites, Latinos, and Blacks. I didn't feel like there were racial issues although each group tended to hang out together when they had free time.

"Okay, it's time to go" Garner said one morning. We got on helicopters that took us to the Cambodian border, and God, it was hot.

We set up a forward base camp. I learned later the normal practice is to dig in and fill sandbags to place in front for cover, creating a small bunker that would be occupied by three guys. For this particular forward base camp, we didn't dig foxholes or fill sandbags or anything. We found indents in the ground and places with natural cover and set up there, three men to a position. From there we did ambush patrols at night, regular patrols during the day. The objective of the ambush patrols we set up was to intercept the enemy as the enemy tried to move forward toward us. During the day on regular or reconnaissance patrols we were out in the field actively looking for them.

Vietnam Stories I Never Told

The patrols were called "search and destroy" or "sweeps" or "reconnaissance." To us they all seemed the same. During the day we walked through rice paddies and jungles and swamps with 50 to 75 pounds on our backs in 100-degree temperatures. At night we slept, when we could, on the ground. I remember thinking, God, I don't know if I can do this, carrying all this shit all day and its 105 degrees and red ants are biting you and mosquitoes eating you at night. It's like there is no getting away from it.

All this time we were looking for Charlie (slang name used for NVA and VC troops), while most of the time Charlie was waiting for us in the safety of their bunkers. That gave Charlie the upper hand, at least in the beginning of a firefight. We quickly learned if we could survive the beginning of a firefight, we could gain the upper hand.

One day when our platoon was ordered to move out from the perimeter of the forward base camp to set up security, Wagner and I established a two-man position. We sat on our helmets and kept watch for any kind of movement. We talked about home and family. Wagner really missed his wife. He was worried about how she would manage on the money he sent her each month.

Chapter 8

The 1968 Presidential Campaign

On March 31, 1968, President Johnson announced he wasn't going to run for reelection. He wasn't running for reelection because the American people didn't support the war, and here we were fighting it. By then the U.S. presence in Vietnam included 525,000 troops in-country, 19,000 troops already dead, and 24,700 new troops being drafted each month.

The Tet Offensive played an important role in weakening of support for the Vietnam War in the United States. Until then, the Johnson Administration had been claiming to the American people that the end of the Vietnam war was near. On January 17, 1968, just weeks before the Tet Offensive, President Johnson delivered his State of the Union Address declaring "the enemy has been defeated in battle after battle" and "our patience and our perseverance will match our power." The visual impact of the carnage in the aftermath of the Tet Offensive televised on the evening news, along with other sensational media coverage, caused many people to believe the United States and South Vietnam were not winning the war and President Johnson would not pursue a strategy to end the war any time soon.

Protests against the Vietnam War spread. They began primarily on college campuses around the United States, in many cases lead by Students for a Democratic Society (SDS). The discontent was further fueled by the draft system of conscription, resulting in 40,000 men being called into service each month to fight the war. The protests were also joined by Vietnam veterans, in many cases severely disabled by their wounds, and the site of these men on national television produced a significant backlash.

President Johnson's assessment on January 17, 1968, may have been correct, but after the Tet Offensive, few were listening. The news media reported that the majority of people in the United States did not approve of the way President Johnson was handling the Vietnam War.

When Gen. Westmoreland requested 200,000 more troops to mount a counteroffensive, the news media reported that the American people had finally lost faith in the military and the president.

On March 12, 1968, in the New Hampshire Democratic presidential primary, Eugene McCarthy came within 230 votes of defeating President Johnson, the sitting president. Normally a sitting president running for reelection is not challenged by members of his own party. However, the Tet Offensive seemed to break President Johnson's grip on the Democratic party and possibly the country. Eugene McCarthy was an antiwar alternative.

Bolstered by McCarthy's success in nearly defeating President Johnson for the Democratic nomination, on March 16, 1968, Senator Robert F. Kennedy announced he would challenge President Johnson for the nomination as well. He too opposed the United States involvement in Vietnam, and his outspoken support for civil rights and social justice issues gained him support for the nomination from Black, Hispanic, and Catholic voters, and young people coming of age.

The conflict in Vietnam was not the only war being fought at the time. The conflicts among Americans, along ideological, racial and class lines were deep and seemingly beyond repair, and Johnson's Presidency was viewed as the cause. His legislative achievements including the Civil Rights Act of 1964, the Voting Rights Act of 1965 and the creation of Medicare and Medicaid were viewed negatively by Americans on the right of the political spectrum, and Americans on the left blamed President Johnson for the escalation of the war.

In the March 31, 1968, speech when President Johnson announced he would not run for reelection he alluded to the ideological challenges the United States was facing at the time:

8. The 1968 Presidential Campaign

> And in these times as in times before, it is true that a house divided against itself by the spirit of faction, of party, of religion, of race, is a house that cannot stand.
>
> There is division in the American House now. There is divisiveness among us all tonight. And holding the trust that is mine, as President of all the people, I cannot disregard the peril to the progress of the American people and the hope and prospects of peace for all peoples.
>
> I would ask all Americans, whatever their personal interests or concern, to guard against divisiveness and all of its ugly consequences.
>
> With America's sons in the fields far away, and with America's future under challenge right here at home, with our hopes and the world's hope for peace in the balance every day, I do not believe that I should devote an hour or a day of my time to any personal partisan causes or to any duties other than the awesome duties of this office—the Presidency of your country.
>
> Accordingly, I shall not seek, and I will not accept the nomination of my party as your president.

In his speech President Johnson also announced that the United States would curtail bombing above the 20th parallel north, essentially north of Hanoi, to entice the North Vietnamese to resume negotiations in Paris to end the war. Bombing between the DMZ and the 20th parallel north was intended to stop the transport of North Vietnamese troops into South Vietnam, which at the time was estimated to be 22,000 troops each month. However, no one in the Johnson Administration actually believed this announcement would cause the North Vietnamese to resume peace talks in Paris. The Johnson Administration was therefore caught off guard three days later when the North Vietnamese did indicate that they would open direct contacts with the United States to discuss the possibility of a peaceful settlement and end of the war. This was viewed as a major turning point in the war and in American policy and there would be no turning back from it.[1]

President Johnson's speech and announcement that he would not run for reelection disrupted the entire political situation in the United States. In the United States and around the world there was speculation that the war might finally end, and in South Vietnam, there was fear that the United States might be withdrawing its support.

Vietnam Stories I Never Told

President Johnson's decision not to run for president caused his approval ratings to go up. Many Americans thought President Johnson's decision not to run would bring people together, that it would be a catalyst for national repair.

Chapter 9

The Assassination of Martin Luther King, Jr.

I think President Johnson's announcement that he would not be running for President had more of an impact on us than maybe any of us even realized at the time. I hadn't been in Vietnam for very long, but my sense of discontent and defeat was evident in my letters home.

April 2, 1968

Dear Mom and Dad,

I think John is lucky they didn't take him last month, if I were him right now I would rather go to school than into the service. He just doesn't know what it's like, if he did he wouldn't enlist any time. It is getting dark so I won't be able to write much more but I wanted to let you know that I am doing all right. Next time you write tell me if Gary is in the Army yet and where he is and what he thinks of it.

Dr. Martin Luther King, Jr., was in Memphis, Tennessee, on April 3, 1968. The city's sanitation workers were on strike and he was there to support them. That evening he delivered a sermon at the Mason Temple Church. His words were foreboding: "I've seen the Promised Land. I may not get there with you. But I want you to know tonight, that we, as a people, will get to the promised land. And so I'm happy, tonight. I'm not worried about anything. I'm not fearing any man. Mine eyes have seen the glory of the coming of the Lord."

On April 4, 1968, standing out on a balcony of a Memphis hotel, Dr. King was shot in the neck and died an hour later. He was 39 years old.

After attending a memorial service for Dr. King the next day,

Vietnam Stories I Never Told

President Johnson spoke to the American people in a broadcast from the White House:

> Once again, the heart of America is heavy. The spirit of America weeps for a tragedy that denies the very meaning of our land. The life of a man that symbolized the freedom and faith of America has been taken, but it is the fiber and the fabric of the Republic that's being tested. If we are to have the America that we mean to have, all men of all races, all regions, all religions, must stand their ground to deny violence its victory in this sorrowful time and in all times to come. Last evening, after receiving the terrible news of Dr. King's death my heart went out to his family and to his people, especially to the young Americans who I know must sometimes wonder if they are to be denied a fullness of life because of the color of their skin.

Dr. King was a Baptist minister and founder of the Southern Christian Leadership Conference. He believed in peaceful protests to fight segregation in the United States, and had a profound impact on civil rights in America, particularly through his speeches. On August 28, 1963, Dr. King delivered a speech during the "March on Washington DC for Jobs and Freedom" that has become a symbol of the man and of his legacy, "I Have a Dream." His speech was delivered at the Lincoln Memorial in front of an estimated 250,000 people. A few of the most well-known passages from his speech include: "I have a dream that one day this nation will rise up and live out the true meaning of its creed: We hold these truths to be self-evident, that all men are created equal" and "I have a dream that my four little children will one day live in a nation where they will not be judged by the color of their skin but by the content of their character."

In 1967 NBC journalist Frank McGee spent a month living with Sgt. Larry B. Lewis of the 101st Airborne Division in Vietnam.[1] The soldiers of the 101st were often engaged in heavy combat, which gave McGee an opportunity to observe them under different and sometimes difficult circumstances. In his documentary *Same Mud, Same Blood*, McGee reported surprising differences in the relationship between Blacks and Whites at home in the United States compared to those in Vietnam. He observed Black and White soldiers sharing supplies, telling stories and jokes, and generally empathizing with

9. The Assassination of Martin Luther King, Jr.

one another. "Nowhere in America have I seen Negroes and Whites as free, open and uninhibited with their associations. I saw no eyes clouded with resentment."[2]

After the assassination of Dr. King there were reports of overt racism in Vietnam, including reports that some White troops hung Confederate flags outside barracks at Da Nang and crosses were burned at Cam Ranh Bay. The Department of Defense is reported to have banned the flying of the Confederate flag at military bases in Vietnam. Southern politicians objected and the ban was soon overturned.

I think Frank McGee's observations may have been naïve and I don't doubt the reports of overt racism in other squads and platoons in Vietnam, but we were still out in the field, and while things got pretty tense, it was just on the surface. We all needed each other too much to let anything racial get in the way, and nothing did. Even so, we were walking around armed to the teeth with M-16s, M-79s, M-60s, hand grenades, claymore mines, and even a flame thrower, so we were all on pins and needles for a few days. The Black guys huddled together and talked about what had happened. The rest of us stayed our distance when these huddles took place.

Back home, in the ten days that followed King's assassination there were riots in cities all across America. These riots came to be known as the Holy Week Uprisings, the greatest wave of social unrest since the civil war.[3] During these riots 3,500 people were injured, 43 people were killed, and 27,000 people were arrested.

Chapter 10

Leadership

A few days later, we joined some other battalions to participate in Phase One of Operation Toan Thang "Complete Victory." Toan Thang was a massive operation, combining the assets and operations of the ARVN's III Corps and the American's II Field Forces, including the entire Twenty-Fifth Infantry Division. Operationally we would be part of the first brigade. The purpose of Phase I of the operation was to maintain the post–Tet pressure on the enemy troops and drive them out of Saigon and the surrounding area.

One day we were out in the field with our whole battalion. We were moving in and out of thickets of woods and small open areas along the Cambodian border. The company ahead of us was moving out of a hedgerow and into an opening. They had a scout dog with them at point with the lead platoon. Apparently, the dog was going crazy and for some reason the handler didn't believe him. They walked right in front of a North Vietnamese battalion base camp and started getting butchered. I saw wounded guys being carried out on their ponchos. There was a guy with his whole stomach missing.

Our company started moving forward to help. My platoon leader, Lt. Meadows, grabbed me and yelled for me to follow him back past the rest of the platoon to a secure clearing. As we approached the clearing, I could see the battalion helicopter on the ground and then I saw an officer by the chopper.

"Yes, sir?" Lt. Meadows said. "I know things are bad for you guys out here. This should boost morale." On the ground were several five-gallon drums of ice cream.

10. Leadership

"Rotate the troops back from the line to have some ice cream." I know it sounds crazy but he really said that. I wondered at that moment if he could possibly not know that there were guys getting butchered back there, guys being carried out on their ponchos with their stomachs missing.

I had only known Lt. Meadows for a few weeks and I already liked him. He seemed genuine and dedicated. He also had this habit of wearing boots with no socks. His theory was that he would avoid jungle rot because his feet would dry out faster without the wool army socks. Several of us tried it but could never get past the blister stage and gave up.

Without saying a word, Lt. Meadows took off his boots and walked over to the drums of ice cream, by then soft from the heat and the trip to the front on the helicopter, and placed his left foot in one drum, his right foot into another. His feet sank to the bottom of the drums. "Ahhhh that feels great."

He never took his eyes off the officer as he pulled his feet out of the drums of ice cream, put his boots back on, and then turned and headed back to the front. I followed. No one said a word. I didn't look back but I wish I had. I decided at that moment I would follow Lt. Meadows anywhere.

By the time we got back to the front, the fighting was fierce. We were only up there a short time, maybe minutes, before helicopters started dumping tear gas on us. The tear gas they were using was also called CS gas[1] or RCA (riot control agent). CS gas burns your eyes and causes your eyes to tear up so much you can't see, burns your nose, mouth and throat, makes it hard to breathe, and makes you feel disoriented.

The NVA and VC carried swabs that they dampened with water and then used to cover their faces. The dampened swab helped shield their nostrils and throats from the gas. They couldn't run when we gassed them, because they were dug in and there were helicopters flying over, so if they ran, they were going to get killed. I only know this from the bodies we recovered later. None of us had gas masks, or any experience with gas other than in basic training where we were instructed to put on our gas masks if there was gas. And most of us had ditched the masks before we headed out into the field.

Lt. Meadows yelled to retreat. That was the whole idea about using the tear gas. The enemy had to stop fighting and that gave the Americans time to break contact and retreat so Command could send in artillery and airstrikes. This battle was my first significant encounter with the enemy and the effects of the war. So many guys' bodies were torn apart as we pulled them back into the woods in retreat. Many were wounded. Some were dead.

After we retreated, we set up a defensive perimeter in an open field and watched as the airstrikes and artillery poured in on the NVA base camp. Nightfall came soon. I am sure there were patrols sent out to recover any of our troops left behind because I could hear sporadic firing through the night. My platoon was not called on for recovery patrol. Recovery patrols were different from all the rest.[2]

CS gas is referred to as tear gas, riot control gas, harassing gas, or irritant gas. This gas temporarily incapacitates people who are not wearing a gas mask. While it can kill, CS gas is generally used in non-lethal concentrations. CS gas was generally used in Vietnam to force NVA and VC troops out of their bunkers and into the killing field, or to temporarily immobilize the enemy to give the United States time to bring in artillery and air support for troops engaged in firefights on the ground.

The 1925 Geneva Protocol, signed in Geneva, Switzerland, which came into effect on February 8, 1928, outlawed the use of chemical warfare agents in war. Chemical warfare was defined in the Protocol as "asphyxiating, poisonous or other gases, and of all analogous liquids, materials or devices" and "bacteriological methods of warfare." In the 1960s, when the United States was using CS gas in Vietnam, it was one of the few countries that had not yet ratified the Geneva Protocol even though it was instrumental in drafting it. This is perhaps a habit or a strategy. The United States had also participated in the

10. Leadership

drafting of the 1954 Geneva Accords, but never signed it and did not support its implementation.

In 1959 the United States adopted CS gas for combat training and riot control purposes. Army Field Manual 27–10 "Law of Land Warfare" in effect during the Vietnam War, provided "the United States is not a party to any treaty, now in force, that prohibits or restricts the use in warfare of toxic or non-toxic gases, or smoke or incendiary materials, or of bacteriological warfare." There were different interpretations regarding whether the Geneva Protocol applied to harassing agents, like teargas, which is generally non-lethal, and in any case, the United States had not yet ratified the Geneva Protocol, and so was not technically subject to the Protocol's terms.

In the early days of the Vietnam War chemical weapons were not heavily relied upon. By 1967 the United States military command had concluded that the expansive network of underground tunnels built by the NVA and VC north of Saigon were almost impossible to penetrate with the use of conventional weapons, so they decided to escalate their use of CS gas. Initially they used CS gas by deploying it into the NVA and VC underground tunnels, to force the enemy out into the open. Over time, however, the aerial deployment of CS gas increased substantially using a newly designed form that was specifically developed for ariel deployment. The CS gas was loaded on helicopters in fifty-five-gallon drums by the 266th Chemical Platoon attached to the First Infantry Division north of Saigon.

CS gas was not the only chemical being used by the United States in Vietnam that was controversial. Agent Orange (a defoliant) and Napalm (an incendiary mixture that burns at a temperature ranging from 1,470 to 2,190 degrees Fahrenheit) played a significant role in the United States' chemical warfare strategy in Vietnam in 1968. After the Tet Offensive, thousands of gallons of napalm were being dropped from and ignited by United States military aircraft over Vietnam every day. Once American ground troops were repelled or pulled back on the ground, military jets would fly over and drop the napalm, and everything within several hundred yards of the drop would be instantly incinerated.

Even though the United States had not ratified the Geneva Protocol, there was still widespread international focus on the legality of the use of CS gas by the United States in Vietnam. The conclusion by the State Department and the Defense Department in support of the Army's position that using CS gas, Agent Orange and Napalm in Vietnam was not in violation of the Protocol, relied on the fact that CS gas was non-lethal. The same could definitely not be said for napalm.

For those of us in the area of Saigon and along the Cambodian border, the use of CS gas, Agent Orange and Napalm were part of daily operations.

Chapter 11

The Monsoon Season

Most of the guys in my platoon got gas masks after that day. But then monsoon season started, and we found out our gas masks didn't work when they were wet. And once the monsoon season started everything was wet, all of the time. So, we did what we learned from the NVA and VC.

We carried a towel around our necks. During the day we put the towel over our shoulders to stop all the shit we were carrying from ripping our shoulders apart. At night we put the towels over our faces so the mosquitoes couldn't eat us, or at least eat us less. We doused the towel with water from our canteens and used it to cover our faces when they gassed us. Most of us didn't carry anything to sleep on except those towels.

April 13, 1968
Dear Mom and Dad,

I just got a letter from Carole and I got one from you and dad yesterday, you can't imagine what mail means to me over here, it makes my day worthwhile when I get a letter from home.

Dad asked about the accuracy of the 45 pistol I have, well I have to say it isn't accurate at anything past 40 yards because it has a pretty strong kick. If I had to use it will be at a pretty close distance and about practicing with my rifle that's what we did at Fort Jackson. The shooting we do over here I wouldn't call practice, but don't worry I am sure I will be all right. We have been out in the field about... I'm not sure I lost track, the days go by fast out here.

The rainy season has started now and it rains just about every day. One thing good about the rain is I have heard the fighting slows down during the monsoon season, which lasts about 4 months. I don't have much time but I

Vietnam Stories I Never Told

will write a long letter as soon as I have time because I have many things to say.

April 15, 1968
Dear Mom and Dad,
I don't know if I told you in my last letter that we are set up in what we call a forward base camp. The only thing we really lack here that we have at base camp is a shower and cots to sleep on. As far as things to do on time off it is the same because there really isn't anything to do at base camp either. It is really too hot to sleep much in the day time so we just try to get some shade. The mosquitoes and red ants in this country will just about eat you alive if they get a chance. When we go out at night I put mosquito repellent everywhere except around my eyes and my lips and wouldn't you guess they bite my eyelids and lips. One of my eyes is almost swollen shut today. I think I am going to get a mosquito net to wear at night over my head. It is cloudy and humid today, it will probably rain again tonight when we are out, pretty soon it will be raining almost continuously.

The geography of Vietnam creates various weather patterns including tropical zones and temperate zones and is influenced by monsoons. The northern part of Vietnam is subtropical while the center and south is tropical. The south-west monsoon from May to October brings heavy rain to both the north and south, while in the central part of the country the mountains provide protection from the monsoon resulting in temperate weather, even sunshine. The north-east monsoon, from October to April, brings heavy rain along the eastern coast and frequent light rain to the north, while south and central Vietnam stay relatively dry. Sixty to ninety inches of rain falls in Vietnam (North and South, collectively) each year.

The area around Saigon (in the south of Vietnam) has a consistent temperature all year round ... hot. The weather in Saigon is either hot and rainy, or hot and dry. December to April is hot and dry, with maximum temperatures around 90 degrees (Fahrenheit). May to November is hot and rainy, with maximum temperatures around 95 degrees, although the temperature reaches up to 104 degrees at times.

Vietnam is also located in the path of typhoons (tropical cyclones

10. The Monsoon Season

of the western Pacific), most likely to occur from April to December. The northern part of Vietnam is most susceptible to typhoons, not just as compared to southern and central Vietnam, but also as compared to other countries in Southeast Asia. In South Vietnam where we were operating typhoons usually occurred only from mid–October to mid–December.

In 1967 the United States Air Force began a military cloud seeding project called Operation Sober Popeye. The goal of the project was to extend the monsoon season by 30 to 45 days over portions of Vietnam, Laos and Cambodia, specifically along the Ho Chi Minh Trail, to disrupt NVA and VC supply routes. To accomplish this, clouds in these areas were seeded with lead iodine and silver iodine. By extending the monsoon season, the roads along the Ho Chi Minh Trail would be softened, landslides would occur, and river crossings would be washed out.

Operation Sober Popeye continued through 1968. Since we were operating along the Cambodian border, the weather we experienced would have been impacted by this project. Not surprisingly, international condemnation of the United States' use of chemical and biological warfare included condemnation of the United States' cloud seeding operations. All we knew was it rained all the time and we were wet all the time.

The next night my platoon was set up in a night defensive position. The platoon leader told me to go out with Saylor to establish a listening post. Listening posts ("LP") were an early warning position, to see advancing enemy troops and signal when they were approaching, so the rest of the platoon would be prepared to ambush. Being an LP was really dangerous since we were outside the ambush perimeter and could easily be caught up in crossfire if enemy troops approached. The risk of getting hit by our own guys was just as high as getting hit by the enemy since we were in the middle of the field of fire. We usually took a radio out on an LP but not always.

I never understood why we would go out on an LP without a radio. How could we report back to let the rest of the platoon know there were enemy troops approaching if we didn't have a radio? Without a radio the only way to signal a warning was to move back into the perimeter and risk being shot by our guys.

The most critical objective of an LP was to remain concealed and undetected. After dark, Saylor and I made our way out of the perimeter and set up an LP position in a clump of bushes. Everything was quiet for a few hours, then we heard a chopper approaching. The chopper's spotlight came on and was scanning the field trying to locate our position. We tried to hide but the spotlight was relentless. The chopper was apparently sent to bring us a hot meal. We heard that later. I don't know if that was true but given all the other crazy things I witnessed it could be. In any case, we managed to stay concealed and the chopper pilot gave up and left.

April 18, 1968
Dear Mom and Dad,

I am sitting inside a bunker right now because it is the only cool place around here today, I can't really call it cool because I am still sweating. I was one of the lucky few that got to stay back and guard the perimeter today. Actually there isn't much to worry about guarding during the daytime because they have helicopters flying around the outskirts of the camp and the troops are on sweeps in all the surrounding areas.

We got a new sergeant in my squad that just got out of that NCO Academy (the school I could have gone to). I think he is ok but some of the guys who have been here awhile resent the fact that he made sergeant by going to that school.

I think Sherri is finding it hard to think of what to write in her letters, I know I have that problem writing to her because we really don't have much in common any more with me this far away. If she still lived in Stamford she could tell me what's going on in town but if she writes about Pittsburgh I wouldn't know who or what she is talking about.

Its funny how it seems like only yesterday that I was a civilian and going about as I pleased and yet sometimes it seems like a dream that there is such a thing as home. Even though I can remember all the things I did and the good times I had before Uncle Sam put the ball and chain on it seems like I have been in the army all my life. Getting out of the Army seems so remote that I really don't like to think about it too much anymore.

If I can get stationed at Fort Dix when I get back I really wouldn't mind the Army so much because I will get a car and come home every weekend. Being there during the week wouldn't bother me at all and being able to

10. The Monsoon Season

take a hot shower and sleep in a bunk with a mattress will really be something to me.

It is the strangest thing with all this heat and walking we do I don't eat much and yet I am gaining weight not much on my waist its all in my shoulders and chest. I think it's from all the weight I carry when we go out it must be about 50 pounds and if I have to carry my machine gun ammo it is even more. The first few days we went out which was quite a while ago I never thought I would make it with all that weight but I am used to it now and I can walk all day like that without feeling exhausted. The first day we were out I drank my two canteens of water by noon and filled them up in a stream I was lucky enough to find and drank those two by dinnertime. I am getting so I can get along on just two canteens a day now.

In the beginning I carried two single-quart canteens and a two-quart canteen, a gallon of water. The platoon sergeant didn't take away any of our canteens when we first got there. I think he knew we would need all of them at the beginning, but I realized pretty soon that I needed to wean myself off the water. I got rid of the two-quart canteens first, and then eventually got rid of one of the one-quart canteens, so I was down to one quart a day. I am not sure how healthy that was but I had to manage the weight I had to carry.

Sometimes Command (officer in the command position at any point in time) would bring in a water trailer by chopper so we could refill our canteens. More often we filled them with well water, when we happened to come across one. We added iodine to the well water. Even so, I am amazed we didn't get sick. Some guys filled their canteens with water sitting in bomb craters and they did get sick.

Configuring all of the stuff I had to carry on my body was complicated. My typical configuration of gear was my fatigues (without underwear but including socks), boots, helmet, weapon, ammunition for myself, one or two water canteens, C rations for two days, three fragmentation hand grenades and two smoke grenades, some C-4 (a plastic explosive that can be ignited with a fuse) and (depending on the mission) a claymore mine. The weight varied depending on what weapon I was carrying, and if I was carrying a radio. I did not carry a poncho or liner. They were cumbersome and difficult when wet. I carried a towel to drape around my shoulders to protect from the rucksack or knapsack straps digging into my skin and to cover my face from mosquitos when sleeping. I slept with my ammo pack or helmet as a pillow. I did not wear a flak jacket since it was hot and heavy and did not stop bullets. While the C-4 was meant to be used for blowing enemy bunkers and clearing obstacles, we usually used it to warm C rations with a make-shift burner made from a C ration can.

The strongest part of the body is the hips. So, I would load up my web belt with stuff. That is why my legs got so strong. I had everything in my web belt except the ammo pack that I had draped over my shoulders. That way I could take the ammo pack off my shoulders and have it right in front of me so I could get to the M-79 rounds, or later when I got an M-16, get the magazines out easily. For the M-79, I carried fifty rounds, and for the M-16, I carried twenty magazines. The best ammo bag I found for the M-16 magazines was a claymore mine bag.

A little-known thing about M-16 magazines is that even though the ones we had held 20 rounds, we only loaded them with 18 rounds. It was widely believed that loading 20 rounds caused the spring in the magazine to lose its tension causing the rounds to fail to camber. We didn't want to find out if it was true when we were in the middle of a firefight, so we always loaded them with 18 rounds.

April 25, 1968
Dear Mom and Dad,

I just have a little time before we eat and then we will be on the move again. We were supposed to be back at base camp by now but there was a change in plans and we will be out about 10 more days, it has been like 16 days since we left base camp now. We have been moving around a lot and now I believe we aren't far from Saigon. The sky is getting dark and the wind is blowing so I guess it will rain again. I hope not because we are about knee deep in water as it is. We are supposed to go on some river patrols in boats in the next few days it will be different anyway.

One night I woke up choking on water that was so high it covered my head and was entering my mouth as I slept. Imagine how exhausted you have to be to not wake up until you choke, submerged in rainwater with rain pelting down on your face. Two nights later, on higher

10. The Monsoon Season

ground, I woke up with a rat curled up under my arm. I carried cigarettes even though I didn't smoke so I could use the amber to burn the leeches off my legs. Mosquito repellent (bug juice), which came in a small squeeze bottle, was also used to remove leeches. I knew if I thought about these things too much I'd go crazy. I learned to shake off just about everything. I had no choice really.

We were operating in an area that seemed to be one swamp after another. It was difficult to find a dry place to sit or sleep. When we set up at night, we always tried to find an obscure spot where the enemy would not expect us to be, so we never set up on trails or rice dikes even though they were the only dry places. That meant we slept in water. Weeks had passed since the last time I took off my boots and socks, and it finally caught up to me.

April 30, 1968

Dear Mom and Dad,

I am at Cu Chi base camp, the camp I took the week of extra training at when I first got over here. The rest of the company is still out there in the swamps and if everything goes all right out there they will be back at Tay Ninh in a few days. I was taken in two days ago because I had a fever of 102 for 2 days and they thought it might be malaria but when I got to see a doctor at Cu Chi he didn't think I had it but he gave me two days to stay here and rest up. Well when I got to the place I would be staying at and tried to take off my boots that's when the trouble started. My feet were so swollen I could hardly get my boots off. When I finally got them off I saw that my feet were swollen on the top and from my toes to my ankles was one big red welt. I had a medic look at them and he said to stay off them and see if they get any better, well they didn't get better so I went back to the doctor and he gave me two more days off and some cream to put on them to stop the burning. I have to go back in two days and see him again. I have a theory what happened, I had wet socks on for about 8 days and nights then I got a dry pair and put them on, my feet were still wet and so were my boots so I believe the dry wool caused it all after my feet being wet for so long well any way its giving me time to relax.

The guy who usually walks right behind me in my squad came in with shrapnel in his arm and leg yesterday from an explosion so I am sure glad I came in or else I would have been walking where he was because with me gone he had to move up one spot and that's where I would have been if I were out there.

Vietnam Stories I Never Told

In Vietnam whether a guy lived or got wounded or died was mostly just pure luck.

May 1, 1968

Dear Mom and Dad,

I am at the service club at Cu Chi right now. I am having trouble writing letters lately, there aren't any good things to write about and I don't want to write about the bad things so what is left to write. I got a letter from Richard Jordan and he says he will probably be over here soon, he thinks it will be relaxing after all the work he has been doing. Well I've got news for him he won't think it is so relaxing when he hears a whistling sound in the middle of the night and the rockets start coming in and once it starts it will go on and off and on all night. I'm getting so the whistling sound wakes me up and I'm up and running for the nearest bunker before they start hitting, of course I never get all the way there before they hit but I usually get a good start on them. Well after he has been over here awhile I want to see what he has to say then about how relaxing it is.

The fighting was taking place about a mile from the base camp at Cu Chi where I was recuperating. During the nights of May 2 and May 3, the base camp received forty to fifty mortar rounds, and there were some casualties, unusual at a base camp.

May 3, 1968

Dear Mom and Dad,

Well my feet are coming along pretty good but I am going back to the doctor tomorrow. If I get any more time off I hear there is a place in this camp where I could make a call home and it isn't supposed to cost too much. If I get there and the waiting line isn't too long I will make the call. I hear it takes about twenty minutes to get through.

May 5, 1968

Dear Mom and Dad,

I just returned from making the phone call that you received in the middle of the night. I knew it would be hard to think of anything to say because I was really confined in what I was allowed to say and that business of saying over didn't help but anyway it put me in a good mood. If it had been a regular phone call we could have talked freely and I would have had many things to talk about.

If I were on a regular phone I would have told you that they have been

10. The Monsoon Season

shooting rockets and mortars in here for the past few hours and now they are doing it in the daytime too. A guy in my company came in today and said our battalion has a battalion of VC surrounded and they killed about 100 of them last night.

My feet are just about cleared up now and tomorrow is my last day off. I have got an M16 rifle now and another guy got my M79. This is one of the new M16s, they call it the M16 A1 and it is a really a great rifle. They enlarged the chamber so the used shells eject alright and it really fires like a champ, I carry about 20 magazines which is about 400 rounds of ammunition and its only about half the weight of ammo I used to carry.

On May 5 I was still at the Cu Chi base camp when the enemy began the May Offensive. There was severe fighting in several areas, including Tan Son Nhut, where my company was conducting operations. Lieutenant Meadows was killed that day. He was twenty years old. He was a hero to me: the way he put his feet in the ice cream that day, how he thought about us, about the war.

The May Offensive began officially on April 29 and lasted until May 31. During this time NVA and VC forces struck 119 targets throughout Vietnam, and except for the attack on Saigon and Dai Do, primarily with mortars, rockets and artillery fire. The timing of the May Offensive coincided with the opening of the Paris peace talks between the United States and North Vietnamese on May 13, 1968. The NVA believed a show of force at the time would enhance their negotiating position.

On April 29 the NVA and VC began a series of attacks on Dai Do, in the Dong Ha corridor near the eastern end of the DMZ. The fighting slowed down significantly when the NVA and VC turned their focus to Saigon on May 4, but later recommenced. The United States ultimately gained control of the area, but the Battle at Dai Do was a very bloody battle. By May 31, more than 300 American troops had been killed there.

In late February, before the May Offensive began, United States Military Intelligence observed a significant movement of up to 50,000 enemy troops down the Ho Chi Minh Trail toward Saigon. The Ho Chi Minh Trail is a network of roads and trails that runs from North Vietnam to South Vietnam by crossing through Laos and Cambodia. The

North Vietnamese began the construction of the Ho Chi Minh Trail after invading Laos in 1959. The Ho Chi Minh Trail was an important supply route for the NVA and VC during the Vietnam War, and was heavily used by them for the movement of their troops.

On May 4, even though we knew they were coming, and most of the NVA were turned away before reaching their targets, 13 NVA battalions slipped through from Cambodia into the area between the Cambodian border and Saigon. The most significant attacks this day took place around the Y bridge (the Battle of South Saigon), and Tan Son Nhut Airforce Base (Battle of Western Saigon).

On May 5, after fighting had significantly halted east of Saigon, it became apparent that the main battle of the May Offensive was going to take place between Tan Son Nhut and Phu Lam where my company was operating. The May Offensive was the deadliest month of the Vietnam War for U.S. forces, significantly worse than during the Tet Offensive. We were right in the middle of it.

Chapter 12

The May Offensive

As my feet healed and I was better able to walk, the next phase of my rehabilitation started, Kitchen Patrol (KP) duty. I am sure the clerks in the rear area got tired of pulling KP and they were happy to hand it off to guys who came back from the front to mend minor injuries. Even though the work wasn't hard, I was pretty annoyed. These guys got to stay in the rear for their entire year of duty, and I was here recovering from lying in water for days and weeks in the line of fire, serving them their meals. Believe it or not I was looking forward to being well enough to go back out, back to lying in water and getting shot at.[1]

I was still at the Cu Chi base camp just before midnight on May 6 when my company and the other Manchus, still operating near Tan Son Nhut began receiving a heavy volume of enemy mortars. Trip flares illuminated sectors of the perimeter of the base indicating a ground attack was in the making. The heavy fighting forced the Manchus to alter the perimeter to protect the six gunships and four F-105s that were inside it.[2] The enemy pressed their attack through the night. Finally at dawn the enemy broke contact and the base was saved.

Later that day, on May 7, I rejoined my company. I left the base camp wearing the same fatigues I came in with and that day I was back alternating point with Saylor and Wagner. The point man walks out twenty to forty meters ahead of the platoon. The stated objective of walking point is to discover if the enemy is nearby or if there is an ambush in the making and alert the platoon. The reality is

Vietnam Stories I Never Told

much different. If the enemy is nearby or if the platoon is going to be ambushed, the enemy would most likely only get a close-range shot at the point man thereby saving the rest of the platoon. Walking point is kind of like being a walking target.

We were given instructions on where we should go when we were walking point, but we had some discretion on the route we took. When I first started walking point I did it because I was told to. Pretty quickly I realized I was better off walking point than staying back with the platoon because I had more control. I decided I needed a strategy, though, so I developed some rules for myself.

I never walked where it was easy. If we were walking through rice paddies I never walked on the rice dike. Instead, I walked through the rice paddy. If there was a path, I didn't take it. The NVA liked to set up ambushes along paths. If there was an opening in a hedgerow, I didn't go through it. It seemed to me the NVA usually dug their bunkers in the hedgerow near an opening or easy place to pass through. I looked for the hardest way to go and took that way. I figured the enemy assumed we were lazy and would always take the easy way. Taking the hard way might keep us alive. When I was walking across a field and heading into a hedgerow or wood line I would always walk at a steady pace until I got to about fifteen meters out from the hedgerow and then increase my speed almost to a run as I moved through the hedgerow. If the NVA were set up in the hedgerow to ambush us, we had a better chance of staying alive if we were on top of them or past them, before they could launch their attack. Their strategy was always to keep us in front of them where they had a clear field of fire. Once we were on top of them or past them we had the upper hand.

Another NVA strategy was to seriously wound the point man. This would reduce the point man's ability to communicate back to the platoon, and the platoon would be less likely to retreat and call-in artillery or air strikes. This was a strategy I later learned was called "keeping them close." The NVA believed that they could neutralize the U.S. military power by "keeping us close" making it difficult to use artillery and air strikes.[3] As a private, I had no control over anything except when I was out on point.

12. *The May Offensive*

In the early morning hours of May 11, we were still operating as a battalion near Duc Hoa approximately twelve miles west of Saigon. We were spread out so that each company had a sector, so it was essentially a company operation from the perspective of the troops. The area included flat open grasslands and patches of wooded areas as well as thickets and tree lines and some rice paddy fields. The tree lines, or what we referred to as hedgerows, were lined with bamboo about six feet high, making it difficult to see through.

We were on a reconnaissance in force mission. There was nothing in the area in terms of villages and civilians. It was a free fire zone where the rules of engagement were to engage any movement and treat it a hostile. We saddled up at daylight and were moving across one field after another and through the hedgerows. Each hedgerow was a potential ambush spot since the NVA could be dug in and waiting. We had no advance intelligence at that point, to know how close we were to NVA or even if they were still in the area. I learned later we were squarely on the Viet Cong's planned path of retreat.

Alpha Company's first, second and third platoons were spread out over a large area, maybe the size of three football fields wide. Each platoon was in two columns with a point and flank. The terrain included sprawling fields with knee-high grass separated by hedgerows of bamboo. Most of the hedgerows were raised about a foot or two indicating the area may have been rice fields in the past.

The left column of the third platoon had Saylor at point followed by me, Davis, then a few others. The right column had Williams at point followed by the rest of their squad. Garner, the platoon sergeant, was at the rear of the column with his radio telephone operator (RTO). As we approached one of the hedgerows, all hell broke loose. Everyone hit the ground. Garner immediately started crawling forward to Saylor to assess the situation. Our platoon was returning fire but not intensely, since we were in columns and in columns no one had a clear field of fire.

As the firefight continued it was clear that our platoon needed to pull back and reorganize. Then Garner got word that Williams was hit and down at point on the right column. Garner ordered me and Saylor to follow him across the field to the right column so that we could get to Williams and then start pulling back. We made our way across the field, crawling to try to stay below the fire coming from the hedgerow, and made it to Williams. He was shot up bad and it looked like his arm was a mess. He was directly in front of an NVA bunker.

Garner was an experienced platoon sergeant with about nine months in-country. He was a Black guy from the deep south with a slow drawl. He was one of the most helpful and caring NCOs (non-commissioned officers) I'd met so far in Vietnam. He really cared about our platoon and he always got in the middle of any firefight. He had already been wounded and had a scar that ran across his stomach, where the bullet entered, and across his back where the bullet exited. After he was wounded, he was pinned down and couldn't be evacuated for over four hours. I think that is part of why he was determined to get Williams out of there as fast as he could.

So even though we were maybe five or ten feet from an NVA bunker, Garner stood up to pick up Williams to carry him back. Saylor and I stood up to help him. For an instant we were all standing right there, directly in front of the NVA bunker. All hell broke loose again. Fire was coming in at us from the NVA bunker in front of us and from the entire hedgerow. I was facing the NVA bunker when the firing started. I could literally see bullets coming at me and passing me, a circle of bullets all around my head. This was so surreal. I felt sure I must have been hit, that I was dying and this stark vision of the bullets all around me was part of my passage to death. Then in an instant I realized I was still standing there and so was Saylor, but not Garner.

We hit the ground. Garner had taken a shot to the head and there was a quarter inch deep gouge running from his forehead to the middle of the top of his head. I looked into Garner's eyes and could see them rolling back. I thought he must be going into shock. I started yelling at him. I told him he would be okay and that we would get him out. Each time I yelled he seemed to look at me, to actually see me. Each time I yelled at him I thought I got him back. I knew he was in bad shape. Williams seemed even more shot up. I knew we had to get them both back to medevac.

12. The May Offensive

I started dragging Garner back by his feet, staying as low as possible. Saylor was dragging Williams back. We were still taking fire as we backed away so we had to stop occasionally to return fire. I was mainly focused on keeping Garner out of shock. As we dragged him back, I stayed in his face and told him over and over that we would get him out and he had to hang on, the medevac would be waiting.

I thought I lost Garner so many times. Each time I yelled at him he responded. I had no idea what I was doing. No one ever told us what to do. I just kept yelling because yelling seemed to work. There was ground fire coming in at us from all over but it didn't register. We were totally focused on getting Garner and Williams out of there.

Finally, after about fifty meters we got back to where other guys from the column were. They helped us drag Garner and Williams back into the brush. From there I kept on pulling Garner further back to the rear toward the "dust off" where the medevac would be. Once I reached the next hedgerow, about one hundred meters from the NVA, and got to the other side I thought I had enough cover so I stood up and carried Garner the rest of the way out, with the help of others. Saylor and other platoon members did the same for Williams.

A medevac chopper landed at the dust off, and Garner and Williams were loaded on. The medics were working really hard on Garner. I wanted to stay with him, to keep yelling at him, but I had to stay behind. Garner died on his way out. He was 21 years old. I've always wondered if he would have lived if I stayed with him. I wish I could have.

I think the battle had been going on for about an hour but it was hard to tell, everything seemed like slow motion. The platoon leader ordered the platoon to pull back. He called in artillery and then air strikes. The jets dumped napalm and strafed the NVA positions. When they were done, a good part of the field of grass between the two hedgerows, as well as the adjacent fields, was on fire or smoldering.

The platoon leader decided we should move one field to the right and try to get through that hedgerow to come around behind the NVA bunker line. He ordered me, Saylor and Michalski to form a line and move through the hedgerow we were using for cover and cross the field into the next hedgerow. The platoon would follow.

We formed a straight line across. I was on the left, Michalski in the middle and Saylor on the right. As we crossed the field I yelled to Michalski and Saylor to stay low. Michalski was about six feet six inches tall so he had more trouble getting low than we did. He carried the M-60. Saylor and I had M-16s. As we started across the field Saylor and I began laying down fire as we moved, and Michalski followed our lead. We were out there alone. As we approached the hedgerow, we received a hail of NVA fire from automatic weapons. We hit the ground for cover. At that point we were in an open field with knee-high grass. Most of the grass was smoldering from the napalm dropped by the F-4s, but it was still better cover than nothing.[4] I returned fire and I could hear Saylor firing on my right, but I couldn't hear the M-60, which should have been firing between us. Then, in some moment of silence between the sounds of all the gunfire I heard a groan that came from where Michalski was supposed to be.

The smoldering grass was starting to burn me. I was still firing into the hedgerow. I looked around for a place to escape the fire, and started crawling in the direction of Michalski. I found a small indent in the ground that was wet, and crawled into it and resumed firing. I still couldn't hear the M-60. The NVA were battering the grassy field with automatic weapons fire. The rest of the platoon was pinned down back at the hedgerow to the rear. I didn't think we could stay there in the open field for long without support from the rest of the platoon, but they weren't coming. I still hadn't gotten to Michalski, who was somewhere between Saylor and me.

Saylor and I both started to move toward Michalski. We reached him at about the same time. One side of Michalski's face was mangled and actually appeared to be missing. He was breathing but he couldn't talk. We dragged Michalski by his feet back toward the hedgerow. We were still taking heavy fire, but we made it back to the hedgerow without taking any hits. As soon as we got through the hedgerow to the platoon, we picked him up and carried him the rest of the way back

12. The May Offensive

to the dust off. Michalski was still breathing when we put him on the chopper. Michalski died on the way out. He was 22 years old.

The rest of the day was a series of firefights from hedgerow to hedgerow, and fire and movement maneuvers in an attempt to breach the NVA positions. All the attempts failed and the jets were called back to pound the NVA positions again. Nightfall came and the entire company pulled back and set up night positions in the tall grass. There was no movement and no ambush patrols that night. We just sat there on our helmets and watched and waited.

> For gallantry in action [award of the Silver Star]: Private First-Class Jansen distinguished himself in heroic actions 11 May 1968, while serving as a rifleman with Company A, 4th Battalion, 9th Infantry in the Republic of Vietnam. Company A, while on a reconnaissance in force mission, came under intense enemy automatic weapons fire. As a result of the hostile fire, two soldiers from Company A were wounded and pinned down a few meters from an enemy bunker. Private Jansen, with complete disregard for his own safety, crawled forward under intense enemy fire, and carried the wounded men to safety. Continually ignoring the enemy fire, he returned to evacuate another wounded man. His valorous actions contributed immeasurably to the success of the mission and the defeat of the enemy force. Private Jansen's personal bravery, aggressiveness, and devotion to duty are in keeping with the highest traditions of the military service and reflect great credit upon himself, his unit, the 25th Infantry Division and the United States Army.
>
> Authority: By direction of the president under the provisions of the Act of Congress, approved 9 July 1918, and USARV message 16695, 1 July 1966

Saylor was also awarded a Silver Star for his actions that day.

Chapter 13

The Longest Month of My Life

At daybreak, I was still sitting in the tall grass looking out at the hedgerow one back from where we had been pinned down the day before. Other troops were just starting to move around. I noticed two guys coming out of the hedgerow. They were carrying large backpacks that seemed bigger than they were. I realized pretty quickly that these guys must be NVA. They must have assumed we moved out during the night. Otherwise, there was no way they would be heading directly toward us. I was waiting for them to get as close as possible before firing on them, but then another guy in our company saw them and stood up and starting firing at them, and then the entire company started firing into the field toward the hedgerow.

The two NVA soldiers froze for an instant, then they shucked off the packs in a single move, turned 180 degrees and starting running for their lives. They were only about twenty meters from the hedgerow, but it must have seemed like an eternity to them with M-16 rounds all around them. They went through the bamboo hedgerow without slowing down. You could see the shape of their bodies cut into the bamboo hedgerow, like in a bugs bunny cartoon, except it wasn't funny at all.

Even though we couldn't see them anymore we kept firing, but there was no return fire. In typical military style it took more than 45 minutes to get orders to move forward into the area beyond the hedgerow, and there were no choppers in the air to monitor the NVA exit. By the time the company moved forward into the area, the NVA were gone.

13. *The Longest Month of My Life*

With no recuperation or relief, we entered a phase of daily search and destroy missions. At dawn we set out to find the enemy, walked all day, set up a perimeter before dark, and sent out night ambush patrols. We were lucky if we got four or five hours of sleep split between us in two-hour increments, before we headed back out the next morning at daybreak and started all over again ... another ten-klick search and destroy mission, set up a perimeter before dark, send out night ambush patrols, barely time to sleep.

The ambush patrol squad would leave the perimeter just after dark and slowly make way to a designated ambush site. Getting to the designated ambush site was critical. If the squad got lost and set up in the wrong location, they ran several risks. If they engaged the enemy and had to call in support, like mortars, artillery, etc., the coordinates would be wrong so the support fire could land on them, and they could also be considered the enemy to another ambush patrol operating in the area.

> *May 13, 1968*
>
> *Dear Mom and Dad,*
>
> *Well I am back out here running around in the rice paddies again. I guess I came out here about 4 days ago I don't remember the time just seems to come and go from one day to the next. This is the 35th day that the battalion has been out and I have been wearing the same clothes all that time. Dad, you're not going to believe what happened I have been recommended for the Silver Star for bravery in action on May 11, I don't know if I will get it because it has to go through battalion headquarters and even if I do it takes time to go through. Well I have to go on an ambush patrol tonight so I have to end now I'll write as soon as I can.*

One night I was part of an ambush patrol. We had a radio for our three-man position that night. The night was very dark and cloudy, providing limited visibility. The designated ambush site was in an area of dense brush and not along a path. This was not a good location to spring an ambush. It was unlikely that the NVA would try to cut a path through the dense brush in the middle of the night. If the NVA did, for some crazy reason, try to cut a path and we tried to ambush them, the limited visibility would put us at a serious disadvantage. If you tried to make sense of these things you would go crazy.

Vietnam Stories I Never Told

As I sat looking out from my position at the ambush site, I heard sounds like someone or a group of people approaching. One of the guys in my squad crawled around to alert the other two locations. There was too much noise to be NVA unless it was a fairly large force. We were all on edge as they appeared to be coming directly at us. We would have to engage, even if we were greatly outnumbered.

As they got closer the voices sounded more like our guys and not NVA. We couldn't tell for sure. No U.S. troops were supposed to be out there. No U.S. troops should have been approaching our position. They were getting closer and closer and we were going to have to engage. I called back to our company commander on the radio. I whispered that we were being approached by what sounded like U.S. troops but we weren't certain. The captain went to work to find out if there was another patrol in the area, and sure enough there was. The other patrol was contacted and told to reverse course, and they moved away from us, still making a racket. We were relieved, but the tension and fear we felt when we thought we were being approached by a large force of enemy troops was replaced by the horror of how close we came to opening fire on our own guys.

May 15, 1968

Dear Mom and Dad,

We are just a little way out from our forward base camp. The fourth battalion which I am with is what we call a blocking force, the first and second platoon are sweeping toward us and we are just sitting here for a few hours. The other night when I went to sleep the ground was dry and when I woke up there was about a foot of water as far as I could see, it took about one day to dry up and it will probably rise again and flood the area again.

The rear base camp that supplied our company was having difficulty getting supplies to us because we were moving around so much. Potable water was scarce. Strange, since we were literally sitting, standing, sleeping and walking in water all the time. The fear of running out of water was consuming me.

On ambush patrol one night, I was sitting guard while the other two guys in my position were asleep. I started wondering if I had enough water. My canteen was almost empty. I started thinking it

13. The Longest Month of My Life

would be okay to take some sips of water from their canteens, and I did. Then I was consumed by guilt. This guilt was one of the worst feelings I have ever had. The guys with me would have shared their water with me, as we all did, if I had asked. But I took their water without asking first.

I promised myself that day I would never cross that line again. This may not seem like a big deal but it was to me. It was a matter of character. Many years later, when I finally told this story, I cried. For some reason it was one of the hardest stories to tell. I still felt the regret. Even to this day, I still feel the regret.

The next day we were on choppers heading toward a landing zone (LZ). As we got closer, though, we could see that the LZ was covered with water. Usually when we are taken out into the field on choppers, the choppers just barely touch down and we jump out as quickly as possible to start moving into a defensive position. We always assumed that the LZ could be "hot." Typically, though, there was dry land for the choppers to touch down. This day, the choppers hovered above the LZ but didn't touch down due to the water. When we jumped off, because of the distance and all the weight we were carrying, we sunk waist deep into mud. Thankfully the LZ wasn't "hot" because if it was, we would have been in a world of trouble trying to defend ourselves.

We really needed a break. We had been out in the field so long our clothes were falling off our bodies. Saylor's pants were so torn up everything was hanging out. That would have driven me crazy. Not because of modesty. I needed at least the illusion of a barrier between me and the ants and leeches and the rats.

On the night of May 22, enemy forces attacked us while we were set up on a trail five kilometers northeast of Duc Hoa. The enemy's ranks had been replenished by NVA that had crossed into III-Corps from Cambodia via the Ho Chi Minh Trail and they were moving back toward Saigon.[1]

Vietnam Stories I Never Told

May 23, 1968
Dear Mom and Dad,
  Well we are still down by Saigon and by the looks of things will be here for quite a while, because they brought out new clothes for us today and that means we will be here for a while. The clothes I had on I have been wearing for 43 days and they were so rotten that they were just falling apart at the seams. We got a new lieutenant today but I don't know if I will like him so much as the old one. I guess I'll give him some time before I form an opinion.
  I have to admit this Saigon area is really a mess and I hope it eases up soon because we only have about 40% of the men we came out with 6 weeks ago in my company.
  We have been so busy lately that I haven't had much time for writing or even thinking about home. Actually I don't miss home as much as when I first got here, I guess I am just getting used to being away. It's a good thing because I thought I was going to go crazy for awhile in the beginning. You better keep those prayers coming in because there have been times I really needed somebody looking after me and there must have been.
  I hope Gary doesn't get orders for infantry training because he will be coming over here if he does. When I first got over here it wasn't too bad but since this Saigon offensive it has changed a lot. I am in good spirits whenever we aren't in a mess which surprises me but I hope I stay that way.

On May 24 in an area north of Saigon and west of the Saigon River, we began maneuvering to screen Saigon and the Tan Son Nhut complex. Our objective was to block any NVA forces attempting to enter the area, and also to stop any NVA forces attempting to leave the area.

The west bank, north and west of the Saigon River was approximately eight kilometers north of Saigon city limits. This was the main avenue of approach for the NVA attempting to enter Saigon. The heavy woods and thick underbrush offered excellent cover. This area was used extensively by the NVA to assemble their troops before moving into the Saigon area and as a point of dispersal for their units exiting the area. They also received reinforcements and supplies here.

We had already taken some minor sniper fire so we were a little bit on edge. Our company's sweep took us north of Saigon through a series of villages and rice patties separated by wood lines along the west bank. As my platoon emerged from one wood line, we could see across a field to another wood line. The field in between was probably

13. *The Longest Month of My Life*

about the length of a football field. The first half of the field was grass about knee high, and the second half was completely open. The wood line on the other side was built up about two feet and lined with bamboo. Through the bamboo we could see the faint outline of hooches forming a small village.[2] There was a six-foot wide path that led into the wood line to the village. There was no movement at all.

One of the squads in our platoon had a new squad leader named Hiebert. He had attended a new program called Non-Commissioned Officer Candidate School in the states after AIT and earned the rank of sergeant upon graduation. The Army started the program because there were not enough NCOs in Vietnam. Normally squad leaders rise up through the ranks and take over as squad leader after being out in the field with a squad for a while. Lately guys in the field weren't living long enough to become squad leaders.

The platoon sergeant told Hiebert to take his squad across the field and into the wood line to check out the hamlet, which basically meant cross the field to see if anyone shoots at you. Hiebert ordered the squad to form a line parallel to the wood line we had just come through and move across the field to the next wood line.

As they were crossing the field to the next wood line Hiebert was moving quickly and some of the guys in his squad weren't keeping up. By the time Hiebert was half way across the field moving toward the wood line he was alone. Hiebert had his machete in his right hand and his M-16 hung over his shoulder. He was headed directly for the opening in the hedgerow leading into the hamlet. He didn't seem aware that he was out there alone but the platoon sergeant saw that he was.

I was the platoon sergeant's RTO at the time, and I was back with him by the first wood line. He told me to get up there to help Hiebert. I started out across the field in a dead run toward Hiebert hoping to reach him before he reached the opening. I didn't think to ditch the radio. The radio was a PRC 25 field radio that weighed about twenty-five pounds and was about the size of a large shoe box. It was about twelve inches tall and about nine inches wide and had a three-foot antenna. The radio was carried in a metal frame with webbing and a shoulder harness. The RTOs were targets with the antenna sticking up over the RTO's head. Unfortunately, as I took off running, I was not thinking about the radio nor the antenna.

Pretty quickly I realized I had misjudged how far across the field Hiebert was, but it was too late to stop. I caught up to him just ten feet or so from the wood line. Just as I got to him the hedgerow erupted with gunfire. The gunfire was intense and was coming straight at us from various positions along the hedgerow. Hiebert was hit almost immediately and fell to the ground.

I flipped the safety on my M-16 to automatic and fired a full magazine directly ahead of me as I fell to the ground. Hiebert was on the ground screaming in pain. I knew I was in the mess of my life. I couldn't tell for sure but I think there was at least a platoon of NVA dug into ten or more bunkers, all pouring out fire. The bullets were tearing up the ground all around me and I could hear and feel the bullets coming in.

I straightened my body to lie flat on the ground and face the NVA position directly in front of me. I thought this would limit my size, making me a smaller target for the bunker directly in front of me that had the best shot. I knew I had to face the bunker straight on but still, that seemed counter-intuitive, and deadly. My head was pointed directly into the oncoming fire.

I reached forward with my right index finger and clicked the magazine release button and swung my ammo bag directly in front of me and flipped it open. I grabbed a fresh magazine and slapped it in with my left hand and smacked the side of the M-16 to release the bolt catch and chamber a round. The bolt catch is located on the left side and can be activated by pressing it or an easier way was to use the palm of the left hand to smack the side of the weapon thereby releasing the catch to chamber the first round and be ready to start firing again. I was pretty efficient at reloading and firing. I knew the only way to gain anything close to fire superiority in a situation like this was to be able to keep firing. Reloading actually only takes a few seconds but I knew I could be dead in a few seconds. Those few seconds felt like forever.

The ground in front of me had a slight rise, maybe three inches, but surprisingly it seemed to somewhat encumber the NVA field of

13. The Longest Month of My Life

fire. They had to rise up a few inches out of their bunker holes to get a clear shot at me. I had to take what I could get. I raised my M-16 and on fully automatic sprayed the wood line from left to right. I most likely wasn't hitting anything since I had my weapon on full-automatic. I realized then that I'd better start conserving my ammo, since I could be there alone for a long time. I switched to semi-automatic to fire a single round at a time.

I needed to take out the bunker in front of me to have any chance. As I rose up slightly to get a clear shot at the bunker, fire rained in on me. I was pretty scared but knew I could not let the fear take control. I also had an adrenaline rush like I had never felt. My nerves were on fire. I felt like my world was a bubble consisting of only me and Hiebert and the hedgerow. I had to control that bubble to survive. I decided that I had to let the NVA know they were in a real firefight and maybe give them pause as they came up out of their bunkers to fire. While I didn't know if I could succeed, I was pretty sure I would be dead if I did not.

I could feel bullets, as if they were hitting my forehead and shoulders, though I hadn't been hit. I knew I had to stay focused and funnel my fear into action. I saw some movement behind the bamboo directly in front of me, and took aim. A head was slightly visible above the bunker, and I fired off several rounds then ducked back down behind the slight rise in the ground. Fire came in again from all sides.

I rose up again and squeezed off several more rounds at the movement directly in front of me, and as soon as I dropped my head down again below the rise, I realized the fire came in again more intensely than when I was up firing. I was forcing the NVA in the hole to drop down when I fired and come up again when I stopped. I decided that I had to pop up, fire a few rounds, and then stay up and wait. The only problem was while I was up, I was a target for all the other bunkers located to the left and right of me.

Unless I could either take out the bunker in front of me, or at least create enough fear among the NVA in the bunker, I wasn't going to get out of there alive, let alone get Hiebert out of there. So, I rose up and fired several rounds and this time, I stayed up. It was crazy. I could feel bullets coming in at me from every direction. After what seemed like an eternity, a head came up ten feet in front of me. I could see the AK-47 come through the bamboo. I took aim and fired. The head disappeared into the hole.

I turned to the next bunker on the left and fired several rounds. I turned again, to the right, and fired several rounds. I flipped to automatic and fired the remainder of the magazine, spraying the wood line. After the magazine was spent, I ducked down and reloaded a new magazine. I heard the radio receiver crackling with the voice of the company commander, the captain. "X-ray 35, what is going on up there?" I had to continue to fire to maintain some sense of control or I would allow the enemy to get a read on me. I held the M-16 in one hand and grabbed the receiver with the left.

"I am totally pinned down, maybe an NVA platoon." I rose up and squeezed off some more rounds. "Hiebert is next to me. Seriously wounded, screaming in pain." "Can you get out?" "I'm going to be dead in the next few minutes." "Hang in there until we can help, over and out." I threw the receiver down and continued firing.

Suddenly I realized that the radio on my back was making me an even easier target for the NVA. The radio was about four inches thick so it protruded well up above the slight rise in the ground in front of me, and then there was the three-foot antenna. I started thinking about how I always kept the antenna straight up for good reception and had I tied it down that would have made the situation even worse. Then I realized I was getting distracted thinking about the stupid radio and I turned my attention back to trying to stay alive.

There seemed to be less fire coming in from the bunker in front of me, so maybe the guy in there was hit or just scared. I decided to try the same routine with the bunkers on my left and right. I started with the bunker on the right. I rose up and fired several rounds and then went down. On the next up movement, I stayed up and waited. The wood line exploded with fire. Then I saw movement out of the bunker to the right. I aimed and fired. The bunker went silent.

Could I be lucky enough to make this work one more time? If I could quiet the bunker on the left, I might have a chance to get out of

13. *The Longest Month of My Life*

this alive. I turned my attention to the bunker on the left. I rose up and fired several rounds and then went down. On the next up movement, I stayed up and waited. There was still heavy fire coming in from the wood line. I saw movement out of the bunker to the left. I aimed and fired. The bunker went silent. Now the three bunkers directly in front of me, and to the left and right were quiet. I knew this wouldn't last.

Most NVA bunkers had at least two NVA, although most of the bunkers only accommodated one man firing at a time. There was a just one small hole in their bunkers, used to enter and exit, and to fire from with their weapons. This was to maintain the maximum cover and avoid detection.

I heard the radio crackling again and heard Wagner's voice. At the time he was the radioman for the platoon leader. "35xray, this is 36xray. What can we do to help you?" yelled Wagner. 35xray was the call handle for the third platoon sergeant's RTO and 36xray was the call handle for the third platoon leader's RTO.

"Get the 90 up on the right and start taking out bunkers. And get the 60 up on the left," That meant have Davis move up with the M-60 machine gun on the left side where he could get a clear view and field of fire on the wood line without hitting me, and get Strickland up on the right with the M-90. The M-90 was the 90-millimeter recoilless rifle that fired rounds large enough to blow the top off a bunker. Strickland "humped" the M-90. He was the only man in our platoon member willing to carry such a heavy weapon. He didn't seem to have any fear. He could be counted on to get in position and make it real uncomfortable for the NVA in the bunkers. I knew Davis would do whatever he could with the M-60. I also noticed Womble behind a rice dike to my left and yelled to him to provide cover, which he did.

I picked a bunker and zeroed in on it. My plan was to take the bunker out completely or at least create fear, whatever I could get done. The NVA continued to pour bullets out of their bunkers but now the fire was slower and less focused. However, the bunkers in front of me and to the left and right were active again.

Picture a shooting gallery with me as the target. The NVA probably felt the same way. I could see heads popping up and down in the hedgerow. I felt like my peripheral vision was on hyperdrive. I didn't think I would be able to keep the NVA at bay much longer. I had to start moving back. By then Davis and Strickland were in position and they turned on the heat with the machine gun and the M-90. I wanted to just start working my way back across the open field to the cover of the rice dikes and tall grass, but I couldn't because I couldn't leave Hiebert there.

I grabbed Hiebert by one foot and pulled him back a few inches, then turned back to fire a few rounds. Then I pulled him Hiebert a few more inches, and turned back to fire a few rounds. Then I pulled him a few more inches and turned back to fire a few rounds. I repeated this over and over again. This was slow and risky and Hiebert was screaming in pain. There was no alternative.

All of a sudden, a cobra gunship helicopter appeared and made a strafing run down the wood line. The cobra was an attack helicopter equipped with grenade launchers, cannons and rockets that could fire in rapid succession. The gunship came around again and fired rockets into the wood line. They were firing very close to Hiebert and me but it was worth it. The fire from the NVA was more sporadic after that. I was about to start inching our way back again when Hiebert jumped to his feet and made a struggling dash to get to the rice dike behind us and to the left.

Hiebert almost made it to the dike before he took another hit. Then he went down, and he was lying there on the wrong side of the dike. This was actually a worse position. When he was first hit, he at least had slight cover. There was a berm at least that provided some protection. Now he was completely exposed.

I started firing rapidly into the NVA bunkers, trying to give Hiebert cover as I inched back and over toward him. The NVA were firing heavily again, but with Hiebert back by the dike I was now able to focus and keep the heat on, along with Davis and Strickland. As I backed up, I could see the trail of magazines I left as I clicked them out of the M-16. I wondered if I had enough ammunition to make it back to the dike.

The cobra was coming around for another run. I reached the dike

13. The Longest Month of My Life

and Hiebert at the same time. I knew the only way to get Hiebert out of there was to get him over the dike. I could get myself over the dike, no problem. To get Hiebert over I was going to have to throw my M-16 over, stand up, pick him up, and carry him over. I knew this was the last thing I might ever do. If there was even a chance, though, it was now, when the cobra was making a run drilling rockets on the wood line. I threw the M-16 over and jumped up, grabbed Hiebert and threw us both over the dike. We made it. We had cover. I felt like I'd made it home, like I'd made it home to the world. There was no time to savor the moment, though, because Hiebert was in really bad shape. He was all shot up and was losing blood.

The radio was crackling again. "What's going on?" the captain asked. "We made it to cover. Hiebert is really bad. I'm with Womble. I think we can get Hiebert out. I don't know where the rest of the squad is." "Get Hiebert out and clear the area. I am calling in an air strike."

Womble and I dragged Hiebert back to where the rest of the platoon was. We got him on a poncho and pulled him back to a Medevac chopper. He was still alive, but he was in pretty bad shape. Sergeant Hiebert died on the way out on the Medevac. He was 20 years old.

The platoon sergeant approached me shouting orders. "You need to go back up to find the rest of the squad and get them to pull back before the air strike arrives."

"What the hell are you talking about?" I was standing there in disbelief. I couldn't believe he was asking me to go back in there. I couldn't believe there weren't a hundred holes in my body already.

"I know you just got out of there, but you have to go back. You know what's going on up there. You've got the best chance we have to find them and get them out." I honestly wanted to say no, the hell with it. I wanted to be done. I wanted to be done with this day, with this war. But I knew someone had to go. The guys in Hiebert's squad were still out there, and Davis and Strickland were too.

"Let's go up and find them" I said, as I turned toward Saylor. He was truly an amazing soldier and friend. He didn't hesitate. We headed through the tall grass to the rice dike before the open field. We looked out over the open field and we could see bomb craters in the open field but couldn't see any of the squad. We yelled out to squad that they needed to pull back. Then we saw some movement and we began laying down a field of fire for cover to give them cover so they could retreat.

Davis was still in his position and he also gave them cover. Fortunately, the bomb craters were at the start of the open field, so the squad didn't have far to back up before reaching the dike. Once they were all back behind the dike, Wagner signaled for Davis and Strickland to pull back as well.

Within minutes the jets arrived and dumped ordnance followed by napalm on the wood line and surrounding area. Cobra gunships came in to strafe the retreating NVA and VC, but most of them escaped anyway since there was no blocking force to stop them. By the time we regrouped and went back into the area, there were only a few NVA and VC snipers, enough to slow our progress and allow their escape. Situation normal.

I think Davis, Saylor, and Womble were awarded bronze stars for their actions that day. The company commander told me he put in an order for me to receive another silver star for my actions that day, but I never heard anything about it after that.

Chapter 14

May Finally Ends

On May 25, we left the Duc Hoa area and established a new forward base camp northeast of Hoc Mon. The next morning, we made an air mobile assault approximately nine miles to the northwest of the new forward base camp. As we jumped off the helicopters, we drew a hail of heavy automatic weapon fire and encountered an unknown number of VC. The battle lasted several hours, and was supported by artillery fire, gunships and air strikes. The VC were in well-fortified bunkers and were putting up a strong resistance. In these situations, they had the upper hand. The second platoon was told to move toward the enemy. The first and third platoon stayed behind in support.

The second platoon walked into an ambush. We could hear heavy gunfire. We couldn't shoot because the second platoon was between us and the enemy. If we tried to help them by laying down fire for cover, we would hit our own guys. We had to just sit there and wait. And while we were sitting there, maybe 100 yards away, the guys in the second platoon were in the mess of their lives. Terry Brody, the platoon sergeant of the second platoon, was killed that day. He was 22 years old. I honestly didn't think the month of May was ever going to end or in any case that I would be alive to see it.

May 26, 1968

Dear Mom and Dad,

As of today I have been in the army for 8 months but it sure seems a lot longer than that to me. It is nighttime and I am inside a Vietnamese house, the company is set up around the house but I was lucky and got to stay inside with my platoon sergeant and I am glad of it because it is pouring rain outside. My company commander was just talking to me, he is really an okay guy, sometimes at night when we are set up in a bad place he crawls around on his hands and knees to each position to see how we are doing, he is just the type who cares about his men.

I wrote Sherri a letter tonight and I am really missing her. I remember the last time I left her at the airport instead of saying I'll see you in a year I said I'll see you in a little while because it sounded better that way but that little while is sure dragging out a long time. Some of the guys who have been here a long time say this is about the worst operation they have been on and I sure believe that from what has been going on.

May 31, 1968

Dear Mom and Dad,

Well I finally got a little time to write and it's about time. I received a letter the other day saying dad was in an accident but it sounds like he will be okay, you don't know how relieved I was when I read the part saying he would be okay in a few days.

I would rather not write about what is going on over here. You wanted to know why I was recommended for the silver star well I really don't feel like writing about it. I didn't know it but that is the second highest award the armed forces has.

For the last few days we have been working in a village and I enjoy it. It's memorial day back home and I guess the old gang is going on a picnic someplace, I sure wish that's what I was doing. Well I'm not really in the mood for writing so I'll end now and write another time.

During the May Offensive, more than 2,000 American troops were killed and almost 4,000 were wounded, far more than the number of casualties during the first Tet Offensive and the worst month of the war. And in the three months since I got to Vietnam, 5,000 American troops had been killed in action.

June 1, 1968

Dear Mom and Dad,

I would like to have you send me something that would be really useful in the rainy season over here. I would like you to go to an Army navy store and buy a navy rain jacket, it is a pullover with a hood and made out of a material that feels like rubber. Some guys have them over here and they are really good because we can't really wear our ponchos when we go out because it is hard to move around in them. Sometimes we go out at night and it rains for a while and we get wet and then it's cold all night. It doesn't bother me if my

13. May Finally Ends

legs get wet but I like to keep my chest dry so the rain jacket would be perfect because it only goes down to the waist.

Things have been pretty good over here today and I hope it stays that way. We have today and tonight off and we go out on choppers in the morning and probably have an ambush patrol tomorrow night. I was wondering what you think of the newspapers I have sent you if you would rather I didn't send them I'll stop.

We are sitting around drinking beer and telling war stories, it's a good way to spend the day. I have made a few really good friends over here and we have a good time when we are off.

June 3, 1968

Dear Mom and Dad,

Doreen said she read in the paper that GIs in Vietnam never get clean socks, well they weren't far from wrong we get a clean pair about every four weeks.

They have been dropping (South) Vietnamese paratroopers in the fields around here, all they ever do is practice and get over night passes and here we are in their country doing all the fighting. Most of the (South) Vietnamese army just sit around in outposts by villages and guard the entrance. I sure wish I was up there jumping with them that would be a thrill of a lifetime. Well in a few minutes I am going to go outside the perimeter, there is a bomb crater full of water, it's about 17 feet deep so I am going to have a swim.

One night I was in a night ambush position with Davis and Saylor. For some reason I didn't have a radio, and that turned out to be a good thing. We were set up along a trail in the brush. There was a path on the other side of the brush, then open rice paddy fields in front and to the left and right. To set up the ambush, we established four positions, three men in each position along the trail and one command position behind us in the center to secure our rear. Think of it as a triangle with my position at the far left on the triangle. We were about four feet from the trail with just brush maybe four feet high.

We were alternating watch. Saylor woke me up because it was my time on. Davis was still sleeping. Saylor slid down in the brush to sleep and I sat with my M-16 on my lap with the safety on. I don't know how much time passed before I saw three guys coming down the trail on my right. There were several ambush positions to my right so these three guys would have had to walk right by all of them to get to my position.

Our captain was in the command position. He was a great guy but occasionally sent out a few guys in the middle of the night to an LP even after we had set up the ambush. However, once we were set up in our positions, we expected any movement in the area to be hostile, so it was confusing to occasionally have some of our guys moving around in what we thought was a secure area. Because of that, I had no way of knowing who these guys were, them or us. Maybe they were part of an LP going out to get in position. Maybe they came from the command position and had notified the other positions they were going out but had not told me. Or maybe they told Saylor and he did not tell me. My job was to ambush, but I was worried they might be GIs, especially after what had happened before with the other U.S. unit approaching us on ambush.

As I tried to sort out what was happening and who they were, they were on me. They stopped directly in front of me and turned to look around and down into the bushes where I was sitting. They were maybe four feet away from me. It was pretty dark but I could clearly see their silhouettes. I knew then they were NVA. There were three AK-47s pointed directly toward me. The tension was unbelievable. I wanted to stop breathing but I knew that was the worst thing to do as it would cause me to tense up even more than I was.

I know they knew I was there. Maybe they weren't completely sure, though; it was pretty dark. But I was sure they could feel my presence. Two of the NVA soldiers moved around the corner of the path to my left with their Ak-47s still pointed toward the bushes. Now there was only one NVA soldier directly in front of me and two to my side.

I raised my M-16 ever so slowly and pointed it at the NVA soldier directly in front of me. I always kept the safety well-greased so it wouldn't make any sound when I moved it. I wanted to move the safety to automatic, which was two clicks. My plan was if my weapon audibly clicked, I would take out the guy in front of me and then swing left to try to get the other two before they could react. If my weapon click was

13. May Finally Ends

not audible, well, I would decide what to do then. Slowly I moved the safety, praying it wouldn't click.

No clicks. There we were. Me with my M-16 on full-automatic sticking through the bush pointing at one of them and the three NVA soldiers with AK-47s pointed at me. I knew I could get one of them, the guy right in front of me. But the other two could get me or Davis or Saylor before I could move my M-16 over to get them. I waited, just for an instant that felt like an eternity. We were all frozen. Davis and Saylor were sleeping. Thankfully they didn't move or snore or make any sounds. I was starting to think I had to make the first move.

So many things were running through my mind. What if they were just the lead element and there were others on the path behind them? They clearly walked right past the other positions, so maybe all the other positions were asleep? If I fired and more NVA were on the path and heading our way, then we could be in for a real mess.

I glanced down the path to my right to see if there were other NVA troops behind these three on the path when suddenly the NVA soldiers fled, running at full speed into the adjacent wood line and disappeared.

I sat there dazed. I don't know why they ran instead of engaging. I think they could feel something but I'm not sure. Maybe I misread it and they didn't feel anything and they simply moved on. I also wasn't sure I did the right thing. I was supposed to ambush them and I didn't.

I woke up Davis and Saylor. The captain crawled to my position complaining about the three NVA having walked past all of us. I told him to go wake up the other positions and if they were already awake ask them what the hell they were doing. I also told him if he would stop sending out LPs in the middle of the night maybe this would not happen. He wasn't happy but neither was I. He crawled away and harassed the rest of the positions. Now we were all awake.

As we sat there, within minutes out of the far-right wood line came a line of NVA like I had never seen before. There must have been 300 of them. By the time we could see the end of the line of NVA, the lead NVA were directly in front of us, about forty yards out, in an open rice paddy. The three NVA soldiers must have been out on point.

We all opened fire. We were the only platoon in the area at the time, so around twenty men and some were in the command position. So maybe there were fifteen of us on the path. We called artillery in almost on top of us to try to even the field. We were able to keep the NVA from moving forward toward us until daybreak when the rest of the company was able to move to our position. Then we started moving forward to engage, but by then the NVA had retreated and carried away their dead and wounded.

I think I did the right thing. If I had engaged then, the rest of the NVA unit would have been alerted and who knows what would have happened next. I'm pretty sure Saylor, Davis and I would have been wounded or killed.

I am also pretty sure the three NVA soldiers on point felt something wasn't right. If so, I am sure they should have somehow informed their command. If they felt something wasn't right, maybe they were supposed to do something, like fire into the bushes at me. Maybe they were afraid. We were all trying to do what was being asked of us, and we were all afraid.

Chapter 15

Attrition Warfare

On June 6, my battalion (the Manchus) were about eight miles from Saigon.[1] Intelligence reports indicated that enemy units were dispersed in the heavy woods and hedgerows in the vicinity all around us. We were ordered to set up for the night. That meant setting up three-man positions in a circle to create a 360-degree night defensive perimeter. This war was a non-lineal war. There was no battlefield with combatants on one side of the battlefield or the other. The war was everywhere, on all sides of us. We never knew from which direction the next contact with the enemy would come.

The next morning, Alpha Company (my company) would be picked up from our night position by helicopters and dropped into an LZ near Route 248. When we landed, we would deploy on line for approximately 500 meters along Route 248 to establish a blocking position.

The helicopters would pick up Bravo Company at their night position and move them to a landing zone approximately 1500 meters to the west of Alpha Company. After landing, Bravo Company would attack to the east moving in a line until they linked up with Alpha. The area would be prepped by artillery fire throughout the night and into the morning of June 6 before we arrived.

Route 248 ran north/south, paralleling the river providing good passage through the region, forming a "Y" with one branch continuing north/south and the other swinging to the east to cross the river into the village of Lai Thieu, in the area of Go Vap. This was the same road and in the same area where Charlie Company was ambushed in early

Vietnam Stories I Never Told

March before I joined the Manchus, illustrating the major problem of this war. We kept going around in circles. After we won (or sometimes lost) a battle we moved out and the NVA and VC moved back in. Success in Vietnam was measured by the body count. They call it a war of attrition. The overall battle plan of the U.S. military in Vietnam was to kill as many of the enemy as we could, and eventually the NVA and VC would run out of men and they would have no choice but to quit and we would win the war. What kind of plan is that?

We were picked up at our night location and air lifted according to plan. At approximately 0900 the helicopters descended onto the landing zone (LZ) on Route 248. As the helicopters touched down, we came under heavy automatic weapons fire from the wooded area to the west and south of the landing zone. Several guys were hit as they got off the helicopters. The wounded men were loaded back on the helicopters for evacuation.

As the helicopters lifted off, still under fire, two of the helicopters collided and were forced back into the landing zone. Both were eventually able to lift off under their own power. Some of the other assault helicopters remained over the landing zone for around thirty minutes supporting the troops on the ground with automatic weapons fire from the choppers.

We took up positions in line on the east side of the road as the firing continued, and returned fire from behind the trees and underbrush. When the enemy fire subsided, the company commander moved us into a defensive position around a building located east of the road approximately 150 meters south of the "Y" in the highway. This action was coordinated with the battalion commander, who was now orbiting the area in a command-and-control helicopter.

From his perch above the action, the battalion commander had decided to change the battle plan. He ordered Alpha Company's second platoon to move southwest to establish a perimeter and he ordered the company's first platoon to move east to locate the enemy firing positions. He ordered my platoon (the third platoon) to maintain the defensive position we had established around the building and provide cover. Then he directed the helicopters to pick up Bravo Company and

15. Attrition Warfare

move them to a landing zone approximately 200 meters north and east of the perimeter Alpha Company was establishing.

As the second platoon maneuvered to the southwest, they came under intense fire from concealed bunkers adjacent to an east/west canal approximately 150 meters west of the road. The platoon leader and several of his men were killed within a few feet of an enemy bunker. Attempts by the rest of the platoon to recover the men was met by heavy enemy fire and resulted in additional casualties. The platoon withdrew to the defensive position my platoon had established around the building, leaving many casualties in their exposed positions near the enemy bunkers.

At approximately 1000 hours a medical evacuation helicopter landed on the road near our defensive position. Several wounded soldiers were placed on the aircraft, and the medevac was preparing to lift off when an RPG round struck the helicopter's tail boom. The force of the rocket spun the helicopter around and sheared off the boom. The wounded and crew were quickly removed from the helicopter and moved back to our defensive position. The helicopter burst into flames and exploded.

The first platoon, which had maneuvered to the east of our defensive position, returned. Although they had discovered several bunker positions, they reported that no enemy soldiers were found between Alpha Company and the Saigon River. The company commander ordered the first platoon to move into the area where the second platoon had come under fire and recover the casualties that had been left behind.

The first platoon moved along a canal, next to the road that ran through the village, until they were able to see the casualties. Each attempt to extract the casualties, however, was fruitless as they were met with heavy fire from surrounding enemy bunker positions. Several guys in the first platoon were wounded in the effort to reach the second platoon casualties and were again forced to withdraw back to our defensive position.

At approximately 1130 hours Bravo Company arrived at the landing zone. The landing was unopposed. Bravo Company moved west approximately 200 meters to cross route 248, then moved another 300 meters west until they came into contact with the enemy. They pulled back to the road to allow artillery fires and air strikes to be placed on the enemy, and then established positions from where they would be able to deliver fire to the west and south across our front. Bravo Company was also able to establish a secure landing zone to the rear and called in medevacs to take out their wounded and also some of our wounded, those that we were able to move over to the secure landing zone from our defensive position.

Throughout the afternoon supporting fires from artillery, helicopter gunships, and Air Force jets strafed the woods to the west and south of Alpha Company's and Bravo Company's positions. The strafing was adjusted so as not to endanger the Alpha Company casualties who were still exposed along the canal.

At 1400 hours Alpha Company, First Battalion, 27th Infantry arrived as reinforcements. They were air-lifted into position by the helicopters of the 116th Assault Helicopter Company that had accomplished the two earlier lifts. Now a three-company force, we dug in and established a night defensive position close to where the second platoon's casualties still lay.

A few hours later, after nightfall, the CO asked for volunteers to form a patrol to go back into the location of the second platoon's contact earlier in the day to find and extract the casualties remaining in the area. There were around ten guys from different platoons that volunteered to go, including me.

We established a column, with the captain near the front. I took up the rear. The column headed out down the road and turned to the right and crossed a canal by way of a small bridge that gave villagers access to the village from the road and then turned left along a path on the right side of the canal and continued in the same direction we had been moving on the road. As the soldier in front of me made the right turn and headed over the small bridge, I spotted a figure walking straight down the road toward me. The moon was out and I could see his silhouette as he approached but I could not make out if he was one of us or an NVA soldier. He had a rifle over his right shoulder with the

15. Attrition Warfare

barrel in his hand and the base of the weapon resting on his shoulder. He had a gait that indicated he had no clue what was going on, as if he had been out of the area and just returned.

I felt it had to be an NVA soldier. Once again, though, I wasn't sure. I wondered if it could be could one of our guys, shell-shocked from everything that was going on. I felt I could not allow him to get past me if he was NVA and then be between our patrol and the rest of the company. I said "hey" in a low voice trying not to have it project up past the captain and give away our advance. The figure in the road froze for an instant. Then he swung his weapon into firing position. I flipped my safety to automatic and fired a burst. He was hit by the burst and rolled to his left into the canal and we could hear his moans. The canal had a very low stream of water that he must have landed in. One of the guys in our patrol threw a grenade into the canal and silenced him. Our advance was no longer a secret.

I have often wondered after that night if I should have done something different. Should I have let the NVA soldier get past me and then be in the path of any retreat we might take? I don't think so. Should I have ventured into the road and tried to subdue him? It crossed my mind briefly but I was concerned my patrol would have fired on both of us. There was no good solution. I have to accept that I made the best decision I could at that moment.

Further down the road, our patrol came under heavy fire as it neared the location of our casualties. The captain and a couple of the other guys on the patrol were wounded, and we were forced to withdraw back to our defensive position.

At approximately 0100 hours, two NVA soldiers moving in from the east walked into Bravo Company's perimeter. Bravo Company personnel tackled and captured one of the pair. The second guy dropped his weapon and ran off into the underbrush to the east. Interrogation of the first guy, who was taken prisoner, revealed that he was an executive officer of a company assigned to the 101st NVA Regiment and that his battalion was operating throughout the area. Throughout the night and early morning hours of June 7, artillery units fired into the enemy area.

Vietnam Stories I Never Told

At first light on June 7, Alpha Company and Bravo Company swept forward toward the enemy positions. Alpha Company of the First Battalion, 27th Infantry were close by. They remained in their night defensive position to be ready to react, as a ready reaction force (RRF), to any contact that might develop.

We moved directly south for maybe 650 meters while Bravo Company moved to the west 200 meters. Then Bravo Company turned south also, on our right flank, and moved around 650 meters. While maneuvering into these positions, neither company encountered any opposition. We found numerous enemy casualties, bunker positions, and tons of equipment that had been abandoned.

The enemy had pulled out of the area hastily the night before. We recovered our casualties without incident. The rest of the day we policed the battlefield, collected captured enemy gear and blew up the enemy bunker positions. Nine soldiers from Alpha Company had been killed.

June 6, 1968
Dear Mom and Dad,

Well I got two of your letters in the past few days and it sounds like you are doing okay. I guess I'll have to hurry up and get home to take over the driving for you although I remember giving you a few scares too.

You asked me a few questions in your last letter so I will try to answer them. I got rid of the .45 pistol when I got the M16 because you don't need it with an M16. I am still happy with the M16, it hasn't jammed up yet and I have fired it after it was completely under water and it kept firing. You asked if they censor my mail, they don't but the reason I don't write about the things going on is I am afraid it will only worry everybody especially Mom but I will have plenty of things to talk about when I get home. We'll have to go to a bar together when I get home and I'll tell you all my stories, they will probably seem more exciting to me then because now it goes on almost every day.

I am certain I did not write this letter on June 6. My guess is that I wrote this letter a day or two later, and used the wrong date. Maybe the date of June 6 was on my mind. That wouldn't be surprising.

15. Attrition Warfare

Attrition warfare is a military strategy with the goal of wearing down the enemy, either by reducing an enemy's forces by inflicting casualties or by causing the enemy to lose interest in the war effort by damaging their morale. Carl von Clausewitz, a famous Prussian general and military strategist, describes this strategy as exhaustion of the adversary.[2]

In 1965 the United States and ARVN forces fought their first major battles against the North Vietnamese. Their superiority caused the North Vietnamese to cancel plans to seize Saigon and instead pursue a strategy of protracted attrition relying on large conventional battles where they had a clear advantage in numbers, logistic and the elements of surprise, and on a larger scale, the guerrilla tactics advocated by Vo Nguyen Giap (general in charge of the NVA). The goal of the North Vietnamese was to use attrition to break the United States' will.

A strategy of attrition was similarly adopted by Gen. William Westmoreland, but with the goal of eroding the North Vietnamese's capabilities, and therefore eroding its will. Body count was the key metric in Gen. Westmoreland's strategy, and search and destroy was the dominant tactical approach. If the United States military and ARVN troops could kill enough of the enemy, Gen. Westmoreland's theory was the enemy would have no choice but to give up.

From 1965 to 1968 under Gen. Westmoreland's command, the U.S. forces conducted this war of attrition. Search and destroy operations were conducted in the deep jungles along South Vietnam's western borders with Cambodia and Lao. In these remote areas the United States forces were able to unleash significant firepower since there were few if any civilians in these areas.

The NVA's initial strategy was to conduct large conventional battles, but when met with superior U.S. fire power, the NVA sustained heavy causalities. This caused the NVA to rely more heavily on insurgency tactics and also to evade battle by hiding troops in, and utilizing supply routes through, Laos and Cambodia.

The United States respected the neutrality of Laos and Cambodia even though both countries had allowed the NVA to establish the

Ho Chi Minh Trail, the main supply route used by the NVA to transport troops, weapons, and supplies. The Ho Chi Minh Trail originates in the southern part of North Vietnam and travels through Laos and Cambodia before turning back towards South Vietnam in III-Corps Zone (the zone where the Manchus operated). The Ho Chi Minh Trail was developed utilizing dirt trails that had been carved out over the centuries for trade between the kingdoms of Vietnam, Laos, Cambodia and Thailand.

While Laos claimed neutrality, in reality the Laos government was turning a blind eye and allowing the NVA and VC to utilize the trails to transport supplies and troops into and through Cambodia and from there, into South Vietnam. The trail spanned almost 900 miles and ran all the way to the Mekong Delta. The Ho Chi Minh Trail was not a single trail but rather a web of interconnecting trails and roads. There was a series of exit roads that could be taken into South Vietnam into each of the IV_Corps. The trail had allowed the NVA and VC to amass more than 200,000 troops and more than 80,000 tons of weapons in preparation for the Tet Offensive.

By limiting operations to South Vietnam, and not pursuing the NVA and VC into Cambodia and Laos, many advisors to Pres. Johnson tried to convince him that the United States and South Vietnam would constantly be on the defensive, rather than the offensive, making it impossible for the United States and South Vietnam to win the war. Nevertheless, Pres. Johnson was convinced not to pursue the NVA in Laos and Cambodia, and instead rely on bombing the Ho Chi Minh Trail at its head in North Vietnam and by cloud seeding along the trail to try to make utilization of the trail difficult or impossible for the NVA to use.

In 1967 Gen. Westmoreland is purported to have established an *order of battle,* instructing intelligence officers to only report enemy strength up to 300,000 troops regardless of the actual number and exclude certain categories of enemy troops to be reported back to Command in the United States. Based on these assertions, some historians believe that Pres. Johnson and his advisors were, or could have been, significantly misled.

15. Attrition Warfare

The concept of order of battle was described by Clausewitz as "the *division* [emphasis added] and formation of the different arms into separate parts, or sections, of the whole Army, and that form of general position or *disposition* [emphasis added] of those parts which is to be the norm throughout the whole campaign of the war."[3]

Under Clausewitz's theory, *division* comes from the permanent peacetime organization of the Army, with certain parts such as battalions, squadrons, and batteries being formed into units of higher order up to the highest of all, the whole Army and *disposition* comes from the tactics and how these troops are to be drawn up for the battle.

The order of battle in the context of the Vietnam War was meant to advise Army units operating in the field what enemy forces they should expect to encounter, so this guidance was focused on the *disposition* of the enemy's troops. The controversy regarding Gen. Westmoreland's purported order of battle seems to relate primarily to the *division* of the enemy's troops, whether certain categories of the enemy's troops should be included or not, in the enemy troop count.

While the United States was pursing this war of attrition via these large-scale search and destroy missions, the ARVN's primary objective was to engage in counterinsurgency efforts in the hamlets and villages in South Vietnam. While Gen. Westmoreland's war of attrition was reasonably successful by body count measures, the overall strategy wasn't working because the VC had infiltrated and were beginning to dominate South Vietnam's hamlets and villages and the ARVN were unable to stage a sufficiently robust response.[4]

In May 1967 the United States established the Civil Operations and Revolutionary Development Support ("CORDS") organization, overseen by Robert W. Komer, a CIA official and National Security Council member. The CORDS was essentially a pacification strategy, the process of countering insurgency by cutting off the VC's access to the people living in the hamlets and villages of South Vietnam. Working together with the ARVN, over the next several months CORDS was effective in strengthening the South Vietnamese government's presence in these hamlets and villages and eradicating the VC insurgents.

The Tet offensive in early 1968 initially weakened the CORDS' impact. However, the massacre of South Vietnamese civilians in Hue in February and March 1968 caused the South Vietnamese people and the ARVN to intensify their actions against the NVA and VC. At the same time CORDS established "Project Recovery," increasing the delivery of food and supplies to the hamlets and villages, and during this period the VC suffered substantial casualties. By May 1968, these factors contributed to significant counterinsurgency gains in the hamlets and villages. By some accounts, at this point in time at least, the United States and South Vietnam were winning the war against the North Vietnamese and against communism.

Gen. Creighton Abrams replaced Gen. Westmoreland in June 1968 and he initially adopted and employed the same attrition strategy, although the losses incurred by the NVA had caused it to shift almost entirely to guerrilla warfare. The search and destroy operations instituted by Gen. Westmoreland did not end but became less frequent, and the pacification strategy intensified.

Chapter 16

The Assassination of Robert F. Kennedy

A few days later we learned Bobby Kennedy had been shot in Los Angeles when he was leaving a hotel following his victory speech on June 6. He beat Eugene McCarthy for the Democratic nomination for president in the California primary. We heard he died. We were too busy trying not to die for it to really sink in, but once again, we couldn't shake the feeling that there was a war going on at home too.

Robert F. Kennedy served as the U.S. attorney general during his brother John F. Kennedy's presidential administration. He continued in the role under Pres. Johnson after his brother was assassinated on November 22, 1963. In September 1964 he resigned in order to conduct his campaign to represent the state of New York in the U.S. Senate. He won the Senate election and took office in January 1965. Like his brother, Robert F. Kennedy was a prominent member of the Democratic party and a representative of modern American liberalism, a form of social liberalism which focuses on civil liberties and equality. Important tenets of social liberalism include support for social safety nets, support for government in reducing inequality, increasing diversity, and providing access to education and healthcare.

Robert F. Kennedy was well known for his opposition to the Vietnam War, his fight against organized crime and the Mafia, his involvement in foreign policy related to Cuba during the Cuban Missile Crisis, and for his as advocacy for civil rights. In 1962, as attorney general, he sent thousands of federal troops to Oxford, Mississippi, to enforce the Supreme Court decision granting a black student the right to attend the University of Mississippi. His relationship with members of the civil rights movement were also tense at times. In 1963, as attorney general, he authorized the FBI to wiretap Martin Luther King and the Southern Leadership Conference, an African American civil rights organization lead by Martin Luther King, Jr., until his assassination, on the basis that some of King's closest advisors were communists. Although his written approval of the wiretaps was for a limited time, J. Edgar Hoover extended and broadened the scope of the clearance and the wiretaps continued for three years, from 1963 to 1966.

Robert F. Kennedy famously argued that life for Blacks in the United States was getting worse, not better, after the passage of the Civil Rights Act of 1964. He tried to find ways to make a difference at the community level. For instance, he sponsored the Bedford Stuyvesant Restoration Project with the objective of attracting private businesses to the predominantly Black, poverty-stricken area through the creation of a community development corporation. The Bedford Stuyvesant Restoration Corporation, the first of its kind, was incorporated to provide programs and services to foster the restoration and rehabilitation of the Bedford Stuyvesant neighborhood.

In February 1968 Robert F. Kennedy delivered a speech in Chicago in the aftermath of the Tet Offensive. Like Walter Cronkite's speech a few weeks later, Robert F. Kennedy declared the Vietnam War could never be won.

> We can and should offer reasonable assistance to Asia but we cannot build a Great Society there if we cannot build one in our own country.

The Great Society Kennedy referred to in his speech was Pres. Johnson's domestic agenda ... the set of domestic programs Johnson established in 1964 and 1965 including the war on poverty, Medicare and Medicaid, Head Start and education reform, urban renewal and support for the arts and humanities. In a speech to students at Ohio University on May 7, 1964, Pres. Johnson introduced his vision of a Great Society: "And with your courage and with your compassion and your desire, we will build a Great Society. It is a society where no child will go unfed, and no youngster will go unschooled."

16. *The Assassination of Robert F. Kennedy*

The night Martin Luther King was assassinated, on April 4, 1968, Robert F. Kennedy was scheduled to speak at the Broadway Christian Center in a predominantly Black neighborhood in Indianapolis. Many of his advisors told him not to go, that it would be volatile, that there would be rioting. Robert F. Kennedy refused to cancel. His words were unscripted and delivered emotionally. Many people believe his words were responsible for the calm that reigned over Indianapolis that night.

> Martin Luther King was shot and killed tonight in Memphis, Tennessee. Martin Luther King dedicated his life to love and to justice between fellow human beings. He died in the cause of that effort. In this difficult day, in this difficult time for the United States, it's perhaps well to ask what kind of nation we are and what direction we want to move in.
>
> What we need in the United States is not division; what we need in the United States is not hatred: what we need in the United States is not violence and lawlessness, but is love and wisdom and compassion toward one another, and a feeling of justice toward those who still suffer within our country, whether they be white or whether they be black.
>
> Let us dedicate ourselves to what the Greeks wrote so many years ago: to tame the savageness of man and to make gentle the life of this world. Let us dedicate ourselves to that and say a prayer for our country and for our people.

Robert F. Kennedy's memorial at Arlington National cemetery includes a quote from a speech he made at the University of Cape Town in 1966: "Each time a man stands up for an ideal, or acts to improve the lot of others, or strikes out against injustice, he sends forth a tiny ripple of hope."

Chapter 17

Phase II of Operation Toan Thang

During Phase I of Operation Toan Thang, which lasted about a month, 218 men in our Division (25th Infantry Division) were killed and 1,156 were wounded. The objective of this phase of the operation was counter-offensive (we knew they were coming). The objective of Phase II of Operation Toan Thang was to search and destroy (we were going in to find them). Army Intelligence knew the NVA were planning Phase III of their Tet, to be launched in late July or early August, and our mission was to attack them before they attacked us.

Phase II of Operation Toan Thang (Toan Thang II) began in June and continued through July. The NVA that were set up outside of Saigon broke contact and dispersed, mostly moving west into Cambodia and northwest into II-Corps. While pulling back, they avoided contact and when engaged, they were quick to disperse into smaller groups and move away from us.

Approximately one third of the 25th Infantry Division's combat forces continued to maintain a defensive posture around Saigon. The remaining two thirds, including the Manchus, were deployed to the west and northwest of Saigon, toward Cambodia, essentially following the NVA as they pulled back.

Extensive and wide-ranging battalion size "search and destroy" and "reconnaissance in force" operations were conducted. The Oriental River was to the south of us, the Cambodian border to the west, the Tay Ninh/Bau Co/Dau Tieng axis to the north, and the Saigon River/Thi Tinh River axis to the east.

17. Phase II of Operation Toan Thang

During the day we conducted cross country search and destroy sweeps, looking for base camps and supply caches, conducting village searches with local officials, and calling in airmobile assaults when we identified a target. At night we conducted extensive platoon-size ambushes along canals, rivers, roads, trails, and other likely routes of NVA movement. Platoon-size roving patrols were used in suspected areas of nighttime NVA activity.

During this operation, we typically operated out of forward base camps set up in a 360 perimeter by digging primitive three-man bunkers on the perimeter. We used tree limbs or whatever we could find to cover a hole we dug for the bunker and then covered the limbs with sandbags. On average, half of us were out on patrol away from the forward base camp during the day and half of us were out at night on ambush patrols.

One night Davis, Saylor and I were sent into a village very late in the night (after midnight) to recon the village to determine if any VC were using it as a base and acting as villagers. It was assumed that any movement would be VC at that time of the night. Once inside the village, we moved from outside one hooch to another, listening and watching for activity. At some point we found what seemed to be an unoccupied hooch and entered it and stayed there listening and watching for movement.

We overhead voices and saw men moving from one hooch to another. We decided they were VC and it was time to get out and report what we had witnessed. It was very tense inside the hooch as we would have been greatly outnumbered had we been discovered. We moved slowly and quietly and made it out of the village and back to our night position without detection. The next day, the battalion surrounded the village and our company went in to find the VC. The VC were really masters at escape, blending in with the civilians and at hiding their supplies, or maybe we just were not very good at searching.

We found nothing and only a few men and none of military age. Most of the men were older "papasans." Our interpreter questioned many of the villagers, to no avail. In these situations, the Manchus were very careful and took a light-handed approach in inhabited villages. The only time we ever "torched" a village was one time when we came upon a small uninhabited village deep in the jungle and close to the Cambodian border. We found VC weapons and ammunition, but no people. We could leave the ammunition and weapons for the VC to recover, or we could torch it. We did the latter.

One thing I always found puzzling when we searched a village is we would find young children and even babies but no young men. There were many explanations for this, though. The young men, even if not VC, may have fled to avoid being questioned by U.S. troops and our Vietnamese interpreters since they would know we would assume they were VC. They could also have been hiding from both the U.S. and the VC since the VC forced many young men in the villages into service. Our interpreters were mostly VC or NVA who had been captured and "rehabilitated," whatever that actually means, so who knows what was actually learned when these young men were captured and questioned.

June 10, 1968
Dear Mom and Dad,

Well today gives me exactly three months over here that is ¼ of my time. I talked my platoon leader into letting me stay here today instead of going on patrol so I have some time to write a few letters. The platoon leader told me last night he put me in for Specialist 4th class that's the rank of corporal only in the infantry they call it Specialist it will be a pay raise of about $40 a month, he says I will get it in July.

Today makes 63 days on this operation and I don't see an end yet. I can't wait to get back to Tay Ninh and relax a little. In about three months I am going to take an R&R and go someplace and get away from it all for awhile, it will be nice to be able to walk around without having a rifle in my hand and everything but the kitchen sink on my back.

It seems like yesterday that I got on the train heading for the New Haven recruiting station. The only thing that makes it seem long is being here and not knowing from day to day what will happen, I guess someday when I look back it won't seem like it was so long but there will be days that I will never forget that have happened to me since I have been here and I will never be able to look back on them and say it wasn't bad, like the times when they used gas and our gas masks wouldn't work because they were soaked with

17. Phase II of Operation Toan Thang

water and we just laid there vomiting and water pouring out of my eyes and my skin burning from the gas and the day my squad was ambushed walking through an open field toward a hedge row and I was only 10 feet from them when they opened up on us that was the first time I was sure I [scratched out] I'm sorry I shouldn't write things like that but I just got carried away.

On June 14, the entire Battalion returned north to the Tay Ninh base camp. Alpha Company and some of the others were placed on stand down status. We needed the rest.

June 14, 1968

Dear Mom and Dad,

We are finally back at Tay Ninh base camp, we came in yesterday by truck on a convoy which took about 6 hours on dirt roads. It really felt good to get back here, we are supposed to stay about three to five days and go back out. That was the longest operation this battalion has had in a long time it lasted 66 days. When we got back they had a trailer full of cold beer and soda and the Red Cross girls holding banners that said "Welcome home Manchus" (Manchus is our battalion nickname). They say we got a body count of over 600 on the operation and that is only the ones we found, they drag a lot of them away I wonder when they will call it quits.

June 15, 1968

Dear Mom and Dad,

Today is our second day in and we will have tomorrow off too and then back out again on Monday. Last night Davis and I went over to see one of his friends who is in the 187th Helicopter assault group, he is a door gunner on a chopper. They have a real nice club with a T.V. and the beer is always cold because there aren't so many guys like at our club. We left there about 12 and came back to the area and the company was in an uproar everybody was drunk and guys were running around trying to throw hand grenades at the Colonel's building or at anybody that got in their way. Only a few were thrown but that's what happens when you push guys for 66 days and then cut them loose they just go crazy.

June 16, 1968

Dear Mom and Dad,

I have been having a good time back in camp relaxing and going to the club at night but it is going to end, tomorrow we are going down around Saigon again. I hope we won't be out so long this time but I don't know. I took my *khaki uniform down to a tailor shop and had the pants tailored and my corporal patch sewn on and then cleaned and pressed in case we go on another long operation and I am ready for R&R I will be all set to go all I need to get for it is my combat infantryman badge but they were all out at the px, they were supposed to give everybody one when they get orders for it but they didn't have any in stock when I was awarded it.*

On June 17, the entire battalion was OPCPN'ed to the Second Brigade (again). We established a night position, then headed south (again) to the Hoc Mon/Saigon area. On June 18 we participated in a combined special operation, reacting to an intelligence report that there was a large concentration of VC in the area. The special operation included a combat airmobile assault followed by a reconnaissance in force movement.

June 21, 1968

Dear Mom and Dad,

  We are set up around a village now, all we have to do is make sure nobody gets in or out of the village, there is another unit sweeping through the village toward us so the morning is easy if nothing happens.

  We haven't had a good rain in about three days now but I expect one tonight, we'll probably end up sleeping in about 4 inches of water and to think that I used to get irritated when I got a little wet from the rain at home and here we sometimes sleep in water and you learn to live with it, A plane is flying over us dropping out propaganda to the Vietnamese people and it has a recorder playing.

  Gun ships are the best support we have over here as far as I am concerned and I am glad to see they are developing them further. Air strikes are good too (that's what we call it when jets bomb) only you have to be back pretty far before you can call them in. I don't like artillery because I have seen them wound some of our men. I was talking to a guy that got here last September and he says this war has changed completely since then. He said when he first got here they were just fighting a few farmers here and there except in the DMZ it was always bad there but now they have got so many NVA down here. He said you never used to see the viet cong out in the open and they would just hit you and pull back, well that has all changed because since I have been here I have seen about 300 live VC and NVA out in the open and when they hit you they usually stay and fight unless they are caught in a completely open field. Things have slacked off for the past week though and I hope it stays that way.

17. Phase II of Operation Toan Thang

On June 22 our company was released from the OPCON assignment to the Second Brigade.

June 25, 1968

Dear Mom and Dad,

　Well I have today off this is about the third day in a row because we have been going out at night every night. I took your advice about writing Sherri to find out if she could come to Hawaii on my R&R I sure hopes it works out. It would really do my mind good to see her for a few days, it would be 5 days in Hawaii and two days travel time. I applied for R&R in August which will be my sixth month here if I get it and she can't go I am going to cancel it and go someplace else some other time.

　I got the package you sent today, the cookies are really great and the socks should do wonders for my feet. Walking around in these rice paddies my socks get so bad I can hardly get them clean.

　You have to tell me if you like me sending the newspapers or if you'd rather I didn't, I've got another one I am sending, read the headline about the Manchus.

June 28, 1968

Dear Mom and Dad,

　I am sitting in an abandoned house outside our base camp with two other guys. We are on observation post, this morning we were up on the roof but it got so hot we came down here where it is cool. Actually I think this may have been a temple because it has statues all over inside and it is bigger than other houses around here, part of it is messed up from bombs. If this was all I had to do every day it wouldn't be bad over here. I just got ⅓ of my year finished. The rest of my platoon is going out on the road on a mine sweep before the company comes in.

Chapter 18

Friendship

I was getting really homesick. We all were. One of the guys in my platoon, Freddy Ferguson, had a transistor radio. I didn't carry one because I was carrying too much stuff already. The only station that played was the American Forces Vietnam Network (AFVN). Freddy could only turn on his radio when we were in a forward base camp, which wasn't very often. Paul Bottoms' radio show "Orient Express" was on, and he played Barry Sadler's song "Letter from Vietnam," and I decided listening to music out here just makes everything feel worse.

July 6, 1968

Dear Mom and Dad,

I got a letter from Bob Hahn, the guy I went through basic and advanced training with. He said he called you to get my address, he said he was wounded by shrapnel from a rocket after he was here about a month and one of the pieces that hit him really messed up his arm so they sent him back to the states and he is doing ok now.

I got three pictures of Sherri in one of her letters you don't know how good she looks to me. I think it made me more homesick to see the pictures.

That's all for now I have a lot of things to do before we go out.

My best friends, Davis, Wagner, and Saylor were still with me in the Third Platoon. Davis had been talking to the guys in the Long-Range Reconnaissance (LRRP or Recon). He decided to ask for a transfer and got it. Recon operated in units of four. They are typically dropped into an area by chopper and then make their way on foot to a designated area to "recon" or to watch. In some cases, it was a perch to watch for NVA and VC movements. Sometimes they were sent into villages with known VC at night to observe and report back. Other

18. Friendship

times they had guard duty at various strategic locations like bridges or even the airbase at Tan Son Nhut airport.

When you go through what we were going through, when you depend on each other to stay alive, strong bonds develop really quickly. I was really happy for Davis but I felt like I was losing my best friend. I think Wagner and Saylor felt the same way. The friendships that develop here are different from any others.

July 9, 1968

Dear Mom and Dad,

Well as of tomorrow I will have four months in-country, one third of my tour of duty. I received a letter yesterday from you with pictures. The house looks the same as I remember it except for new paint, which really does a lot for it, I sure can't wait to see that house again.

We are staying in camp tonight and going out on a sweep tomorrow. We have been working one day and a night out and a day and a night in camp on bunker guard. The place we are set up in is only about 2 miles from Tan Su Nhut airport, which is right outside Saigon. We are supposed to be here for a month or two, we are part of the Saigon Defense plan which takes in three divisions all set up around Saigon waiting for the next offensive to start against Saigon, it is expected to start in a few days but they could be wrong. Every day we watch the jet leaving the airport taking men to R&R and some of them going to the states. We call the TWA jets freedom birds because they are the ones going to San Francisco. I don't know if I ever told you the expression used when we talk about going home the guys say when I get to the world instead of saying when I get home, I guess that's because this place is so different than the rest of the world that it almost seems like another planet. We have been doing a lot of work on our bunker and making fighting provisions, by now we must have filled about 900 sandbags for this bunker.

My orders still haven't come through for corporal but that is Vietnam for you they are probably held up someplace. Last time we were at Tay Ninh one guy got awarded a bronze star that he was put in for in February so it was almost four months later.

They gave us a pay raise, at the grade I am at now which is E-3 I got about $15 more a month and when I get my orders for E-4 I will be making about $190 base pay plus $65 combat pay. You know what bothers me is everybody stationed in Vietnam gets the $65 combat pay but only 1 out of 5 of us are combat troops, I think they should give the guys that are actually doing the fighting a little more than the guys who just sit back at base camp and push a pencil or work in supply.

Vietnam Stories I Never Told

Dwight Davis volunteered for a recon team and he left the other day and things don't seem the same around here anymore, we were good friends and used to sit around and talk every night we were in camp. He had been in Germany and had a lot to tell about it.

I took the M-60 a few weeks after Davis transferred, and carried it for about a month. The M-60 or "the gun" as it was known was heavy and the ammunition was heavy. I carried 300 rounds and other guys in the platoon carried another 100 rounds. The M-60 was an excellent weapon, very accurate. The only problem was that the M-60s the army had were in many cases very old and not well maintained. They would jam often with a round stuck in the chamber. That required the gunner to pull the ammo belt and stick a cleaning rod down the barrel to extract the shell. In the worst case it could require a new barrel. That extreme situation never happened to me. Also, sometimes the M-60 wouldn't chamber a round. That was easier to fix with a reload.

I kept the M-60 clean, well-oiled and greased and it still jammed occasionally. How were the problems with the M-60 and the other weapons we carried so well-known and yet nothing was done about it? We had a weapon that could clearly save us in a firefight when it worked. The ones we had only worked some of the time, meaning we could only hope it would work when we were in the middle of a firefight, not the kind of help we needed. Our requests for a replacement and repair went unheeded.

Not long after Davis left, we moved to a new location and established a new forward base camp outside Saigon in the Ho Bo woods. Things quieted down. We were there to protect Saigon from another NVA attack, guarding a bridge on a road leading to Saigon not far from our forward base camp. The villagers got used to our presence there and it felt good to let down our guard a little. Young teenage girls would hang around and flirt with us. It was very innocent. I think we all enjoyed the feeling of just being kids again. And we definitely enjoyed the feeling of being out of harm's way, even if only temporarily.

One day Wagner and I were invited into a Vietnamese wedding reception taking place at a gathering place, like a hall, nearby. There were enough guys guarding the bridge, so we accepted the invitation.

18. Friendship

The reception was a festive affair with lots of sake, toasts in Vietnamese and singing. Many of the guests were dressed in brightly colored outfits. They were very welcoming.

In most cultures, marriage is a significant cultural event and includes many symbolic rites, primarily derived from or informed by the religious teachings of the community of the bride and groom's family. For Buddhists, to which most people in the hamlets and villages of South Vietnam ascribed, marriage was a secular affair, meaning that marriage is not a religious obligation or commitment. As a result, a Buddhist marriage ceremony itself is a simple joyful occasion that celebrates the partners joining in marriage. The Vietnamese marriage ceremony also incorporates Confucian ideology, which is sometimes viewed as a religion and sometimes viewed as a philosophy. A guiding principle of Confucianism is that human beings are fundamentally good, and its main idea is the importance of an individual having good moral character.

A traditional Vietnamese wedding includes six separate ceremonies. Well into the twentieth century Vietnamese weddings were arranged and in many cases the bride and groom had never even met, so the first of the six ceremonies, the Nap Tai, revolved around the introduction of the bride and groom to each other and their families. During this first ceremony, the groom's family informs the bride's family that the groom intends to ask the bride to marry him by bringing a pair of birds to the bride's family home. This was followed by the second ceremony, the Van Danh, when the groom sends a matchmaker to the bride's home to ask for the bride's name and birthday.

The groom informs the bride's family in the third ceremony, the Nap Cat, that he has met with a fortune teller and the fortune teller said he and the bride would make a good couple. If the fortune teller does not think the bride and groom would make a good couple, there would be no marriage. The groom and the groom's family bring presents to the bride's family during the fourth ceremony, the Nap Te. The fifth ceremony, the Thinh Ky, is held to decide on the wedding date. The wedding date is a very important decision in Vietnamese culture and is usually decided by the fortune teller. Once the date is decided, no one in the groom's family can be late to the ceremony, or not attend the ceremony, since doing so will bring bad luck to the marriage.

The sixth ceremony, the Than Nghinh, is the actual wedding ceremony. The groom's family bring presents to the bride's family and escorts the bride back to the groom's house. Before they leave the bride's house, the bride and groom pray to an altar to ask their ancestors for permission to marry and then thank both sets of parents for raising them and protecting them. Then they exchange rings and receive gifts. After they arrive at the groom's house, there is a celebration that includes a band, and guests sing wedding songs on stage to bring luck to the married couple. In the middle of the celebration the bride and groom go to each table to be congratulated and receive money.

The wedding we attended was obviously in this sixth, or final, stage. We only stayed for a little while, but this was an enjoyable and memorable respite. Even though at the time I felt honored to be invited to the celebration, I didn't recognize the significance of the invitation. Looking back, I think including us in the celebration, given what was happening all around them and all around us, was an indication of their trust in us, and their support, at least at this time, and in this village.

Wagner and I also decided to take an unauthorized trip, otherwise known as AWOL (absent without leave) into Saigon. We caught a taxi for the trip. The taxis in the Nam were three-wheel vehicles with one wheel in front and two in the rear. Somehow we convinced the driver to let us take turns driving and we came close to destroying his vehicle. In Saigon we walked around and went to bars, nothing very exciting but I am glad we went.

July 15, 1968

Dear Mom and Dad,

Well the First Sergeant told me I didn't get the R&R to Hawaii so I wrote and told Sherri. I don't think I told you but she said she would meet me there

18. Friendship

Herbert Jansen and Charles Wagner, near Saigon, July 1968.

if I got the R&R. I am disappointed but I am not letting it get me down. I hope Sherri takes it okay. I guess in a few months I will try to get someplace like Hong Kong or Australia.

One of the guys that came out from Tay Ninh said they have orders for me back at Tay Ninh. He said it is the orders for the silver star I was recommended for but I am not going to believe it until I see it. He said he thinks they have orders for my promotion also, they usually hold all the orders back until they have a few and then bring them out all at once.

About the Army letting me out if they served over here and only have five months left in the Army, I will have seven months left when I leave here and I don't think I will extend for two months over here to get my discharge five months early, I will be happy to make it through 12 months without pushing my luck and extending for two more. Another thing is they say I have a good chance of making sergeant over here and then I won't mind the Army back in some fort in the States chasing new trainees around. I thought my drill instructor was hard on us, wait until I get my chance, I'll have the time of my life.

Vietnam Stories I Never Told

July 24, 1968

Dear Mom and Dad,

I just got the rain jacket you sent and it came just at the right time, it is getting so it rains almost continuously the last few days and it will stay that way until about the end of August. I really appreciate that you sent the jacket so fast.

We are still set up outside Saigon and everything is still going okay. The enemy is supposed to be planning another offensive on Saigon and they have been having meetings in the villages at night but somehow the army has gotten a lot of tips and we have been going in and picking them up at the meetings so maybe we will be able to stop the offensive.

The other night we were sitting in our bunker and it was pouring rain we were all dead tired from walking all day and one of the guys said I wonder what it would feel like to take a hot shower and crawl into bed with clean sheets it was something to look at the expressions on the guys faces like they couldn't imagine what it would be like. That makes me home sick talking about things like that so I try not to talk about it too often.

July 30, 1968

Dear Mom and Dad,

You don't know how much I am starting to miss being home it just grows on me as the days go on. You asked if there is anything else I would like well the cookies sound great but I can't think of anything else I can use. Well I guess I'll end for now say hello to Ester and ask her to keep a beer cold for me for when I get home. I miss you all very much, keep writing I really look forward to your letters.

From June 1 to July 31, 145 men in our division were killed in action and 879 men were wounded.

Chapter 19

The August Offensive

Phase III of the Tet Offensive (also known as the August Offensive) began on August 17, 1968. The Tay Ninh Province close to the Cambodian border was the main area of the NVA and VC operations during this offensive. And just like the May Offensive, we were right in the middle of it.

August 4, 1968
Dear Mom and Dad,
Today we are working in a village not far from our camp. We are supposed to be helping the villagers build things in the village. Nothing has been happening around Saigon for a long time and we have to stay here to guard it so I guess they figured we might as well be doing something constructive. We are going to start doing this one-day a week from now on. There is a rumor around that we will be staying in this base camp until November but that is hard for me to believe that we will stay that long, I sure hope we do because we have the camp set up now and we haven't made contact in a long time so unless they start another offensive of Saigon it should be pretty good. Except for all the walking on sweeps and carrying a weapon and ammunition it almost seems as if there isn't a war going on anymore.
I got a letter from Sergeant Davis the other day he is one of my old buddies that left A company about three weeks ago to go to the recon platoon. He said they were set up right outside Tan Su Nut air force base and they don't do anything except go to the air force PX boy he really rubbed it in.
Our platoon is built up bigger than I have ever seen it; it makes it easier on everybody with more men. I was just thinking there are only 6 guys in our platoon out of 34 that were here when I got to the company. By the time you get this letter I will have 5 months in-country and be working on my 6th month really sounds good I can't wait to be half way home. Before I end there is one thing I want to ask you the next time you send me a package send two

shaving brushes because I lost the other one you sent me when I first came over and they are really good for cleaning weapons.

August 9, 1968

Dear Mom and Dad,

Sgt Davis came around to talk to Wagner and I it was amazing how much better a guy looks after just a few weeks off the line, all the worry that builds up in a guy when he is on the line isn't noticeable until you see him after a few weeks of taking it easy. I guess it's because you live with them day to day and you just don't notice. He has gained weight and his face doesn't have that drawn look the guys out here get. You probably think that a recon platoon would be worse than being in a line company but they are too small for combat missions so they mostly pull security and once in a while set up an ambush.

August 16, 1968

Dear Mom and Dad,

I have been thinking that if I extended my tour over here for 45 days that I would be discharged from the army when I went home which would be sometime in the end of April if I extended, only 8 months from now. It would be great to get out then and be home for the summer but I won't do it if I am still serving up on the line because it's not worth the chance, if I get a job back at base camp like a lot of guys get after they have been here nine or ten months I may do it. As long as you are back in Tay Ninh there really isn't much to worry about. I won't decide until I get a job in the rear.

I don't think I told you I am a gunner now, I carry an m60 machine gun which weighs about 30 pounds, when I have 100 rounds of ammunition attached in the assault bag, I carry 300 rounds and I have three ammo bearers that carry 200 rounds each. After I gave up being a radio man I wanted the machine gun. That was about three weeks ago. It is the safest job I have had since I got here. For the first three months I walked point (that is the first man in the file which isn't exactly the best place to be) then I was radio man for the platoon leader and he walks up front. So now I walk in the middle of the file. It's a great weapon to have especially when you are set up in the middle of no place at night no Charlie (that's viet cong) is going to run through a machine gun.

The August Offensive was conducted in two waves; the first wave ended on August 31 and the second wave started on September 11 and

19. The August Offensive

ended on September 27. Saylor was wounded in the early days of the first wave. Command had been rotating guys in and out of their units on short-term assignments. I am pretty sure Saylor was temporarily assigned to the signal corps on Black Virgin Mountain about ten kilometers northeast of Tay Ninh when the NVA and VC initiated their August Offensive.

The 121st Signal Battalion established a radio relay station on top of Black Virgin Mountain in 1966 and maintained control of the top of the mountain throughout most of the war. Interestingly, the VC controlled the bottom of the mountain and the surrounding area, so the base could only be reached by helicopter. On May 13 during the May offensive the base was overrun by VC but the United States took back control the following day. Twenty-four U.S. troops were killed during those 24 hours on Black Virgin Mountain. Given the importance of the radio relay station to the United States and South Vietnamese forces, Black Virgin Mountain was always in the NVA and VC's crosshairs.

I don't know exactly what happened to Saylor. I never saw him again. I know he survived his wounds and shipped home, back to the world. I think about him often, and about how many times we helped each other stay alive.

On August 21, Alpha Company was conducting operations in Gia Dinh Province. One of our guys was killed. He wasn't in my platoon, so I didn't know him very well. Platoons were like silos, very separate and isolated from each other. The guys in your platoon were the guys who were depending on you, and you were depending on them, so they were the guys you really knew.

August 21, 1968
Dear Mom and Dad,

They moved the recon platoon into the base camp so I have seen Davis a few times in the last few days.

Things are getting started again but it isn't too bad yet, I knew it couldn't last forever. We have been here for 63 days now, two more days and it will be as long as the last operation. This operation doesn't seem half as long as the last one because we have had it pretty good this time. I had a picture I forgot to send the last time the guy in the middle is our medic he has lasted the longest out of the rest of them the last operation we had three medics wounded in our platoon.

On August 24, still operating in the Gia Dinh Province another guy in our company was killed. The atmosphere was getting very tense. We were all worried. After what we'd been through, it was like it was all starting again, and no one would say it but we were scared.

August 28, 1968
Dear Mom and Dad,

I was supposed to go out this morning on choppers but they didn't have enough room so six of us had to stay back at base camp. It really broke my heart. Well I won't have to go out until 3 o'clock when they bring out a resupply to the company for tonight. They are in the swamps today so I'm glad I am not out there. Being out there tonight with all the mosquitoes in the swamps should be fun you can coat yourself with insect repellent and the mosquitoes still drive you crazy. I think they do the backstroke on repellent. We had one guy that came in about three weeks ago and he used to get so mad at the mosquitoes that he would start yelling at them in the middle of the night and you just can't go around yelling in the middle of the night over here. Then one night we set up an ambush on a trail and this guy wanted to go out and sleep on the trail we were going to ambush if anybody came down it. Well the platoon leader got sick of him and put him on permanent KP and now I hear that he may get a discharge because he even messes up on KP. Maybe he is not so stupid after all.

Davis came around the other day with a 25th Division paper and told me it had my name in it for my award. He is in it also for a bronze star he was there the day I was put in for it and he was wounded that day but it wasn't bad just a piece of shrapnel in the nose.

I am going to send part of the newspaper with this letter; it has a list of the men who won awards I guess it's for the last operation the one that lasted for 67 days.

Chapter 20

The Silver Star

On September 1, 1968, Saylor and I were physically awarded the silver star. The silver star can only be awarded in person by the commander in theater who is at least a three-star general. On that day, it must have been Gen. F.K. Mearns, although I don't specifically recall. I think he was replaced a few days later by Gen. Ellis Williamson.

September 1, 1968

Dear Mom and Dad,

Well would you believe I finally got my silver star. I had the Star pinned on me by the general and our first Sergeant took a few pictures of it. When he has them developed I'll send a few home. I didn't get the certificate that goes with it because the company puts it into a special folder. It will probably be held at Tay Ninh and I can get it when we go in. One of the guys was telling me that the army writes to the hometown papers about things like that.

September 2, 1968

Dear Mom and Dad,

Well I decided to just put my star in an envelope and send it home instead of running around with it over here. I asked the first sergeant about the certificate that goes along with it and the ribbon I wear on my dress uniform and he said they are in Tay Ninh and I can pick them up when we go. They probably have a box to put it in that I will get too but they figure all that stuff will only get messed up out here.

I always thought it would be all silver but it has the little silver stat in the center (read the inscription on the back).

Just 8 more days and I have 6 months.

Award Ceremony—Award of the Silver Star to Herbert G. Jansen, September 1968, near Tay Ninh.

September 4, 1968

Dear Mom and Dad,

I put in for an R&R or a 7-day leave to a place called Taipei for October and I got the 7-day leave. It starts October 1 and ends Oct 7. The only thing different between R&R and a 7-day leave is on R&R you are guaranteed a seat on the plane and leave is a space availability deal on the flights, something like standby. But if I can't get a seat on a plane to Taipei I will probably be able to get on a flight to another R&R location like Bangkok or Australia there is always an extra seat going to someplace and with a leave you can go anyplace as long as you get a seat on a plane.

Significant enemy activity began to occur south of Saigon between Highway 22 and Highway 26. The 25th Infantry Division initiated a

19. The Silver Star

About GIs

Stamford Soldier A Hero

TAY NINH, Vietnam — Crawling forward under a hail of enemy fire, the young Stamford, Conn. soldier reached his wounded comrade and carried him to safety. He then returned and rescued another wounded man.

For gallantry in action that day, Army Spec. 4 Herbert G. Jansen, son of George Jansen, 219 Courtland Ave., Stamford, received the Silver Star Medal in ceremonies near Tay Ninh Sept. 11.

The incident occurred last May 11 while Spec. Jansen was serving as a rifleman on a reconnaissance mission. When his unit came under heavy enemy fire, the two soldiers from his company were hit and pinned down a few yards from a Viet Cong bunker.

Spec. Jansen is assigned to Company A, 4th Battalion, of the 25th Infantry Division's 9th Infantry.

Stamford [CT] *Advocate* (hometown newspaper) reporting the award of the Silver Star to Herbert G. Jansen (September 11; date in article is incorrect).

large operation in this area on Sept 5 and there were several enemy contacts over the next days. Then all available troops were repositioned because intelligence reports indicated that Tay Ninh City would be attacked between September 10 and September 15.

September 9, 1968

Dear Mom and Dad,

Well I have a big shock for you, Sherri and I are going to be married June 21, 1969 if everything works out alright. Sherri wanted to set a date for quite awhile now and I finally gave in and I guess it is what I wanted to do but I was just holding out for some reason. Maybe I am doing the wrong thing not waiting until I get home before making the decision but it is what I want and I think it will work out.

As of tomorrow I will finally reach the half way point. I have been waiting to get that far for what seems like an awful long time.

The ground is dry in the area we are in and my feet are finally clearing up. They have given me trouble for months now.

September 12, 1968

Dear Mom and Dad,

Wagner leaves here March 3 and I leave the 10th so we may be sent to the same post because that's the way they have been working it, all the guys leaving in one month go to one post and the next month they go to another one. If we get stationed together we will probably be busted to E-1 before long the way we mess around when they let us loose. When things get bad he is one of the few guys who will be around when you need him.

September 14, 1968

Dear Mom and Dad,

Today Wagner and I caught a ride and went over to where the recon platoon is set up. We asked for Davis and they told us he had been wounded and was in a hospital in Japan. It kind of got to us because we were pretty close friends and now Wagner and I are the only two left out of our old squad when we first got here.

Well I really don't have much to say I guess I have been over here so long I don't have much to say except what goes on over here and that isn't worth talking about.

During this phase Saigon was struck again, however the attacks were sporadic and the NVA and VC were easily turned back. Still, 700 United States troops were killed and many more than that were wounded.

September 17, 1968

Dear Mom and Dad,

I don't have much time to write today. I got the pictures back from the awards ceremony and a few others I figured I would send home. I'm all ready for my leave. Things are still going all right over here. I am sorry it's so short but I have to go.

19. The Silver Star

September 19, 1968

Dear Mom and Dad,

    We are just sitting around this morning so I decided I would write and let you know I am still kicking. We don't have to go out until 1 o'clock today. Every once in awhile we just go out and pull security at the bridge going into Saigon. I wish I did that every day (what a life).

    I wrote Davis a letter today. I am going to mail it to recon and hope they forward it to him. I heard he had a chest wound but is doing alright. It isn't the same for me and Wagner with Davis gone as far as we are concerned he was the best squad leader Vietnam ever had.

September 24, 1968

Dear Mom and Dad,

    I am going in tomorrow to get ready to go on my leave. It will probably be around the 12th of next month before I go out to the field again. By the way tomorrow I will have one year in the army. I gave my machine gun to another guy and I don't think I will carry it when I get back (from leave). I like the machine gun and love the way it fires but there is one thing I don't like about it, that is I had to depend on other people to carry ammo for me, I carried 300 rounds and I had three guys who always walked behind me carrying 200 rounds each but some guys don't like to get up to bring the ammo over, so I guess I'll go back to the M16 again.

Chapter 21

Rest and Relaxation

Most people who know anything about Vietnam have heard of R&R, which was short for Rest & Relaxation. It was a four-day trip to various locations outside the Nam that did not count against leave time. What most people don't know is that getting R&R is very difficult for the grunts in the field like me. I applied in April, May and June and did not get one. Other guys in my unit had the same experience. It seemed to us the only ones getting R&R were the clerks and other guys in the rear-area base camps. So, I decided to request a leave.

On October 1, I made my way to Tan Son Nhut to catch a flight. The big difference with leave and R&R is that with R&R the trip arrangements were in the order including the destination such as Hawaii, Taipei, Hong Kong, etc. With a leave you had to go standby. And a leave is counted as leave time against the 30 days of leave allowed annually—but R&R is not counted against the 30 days. At first, I wanted to go to Hawaii because I had it in my head that Sherri could meet me there, which was pretty unrealistic since she was a senior in high school. Then I decided to try to go to Taipei. I couldn't get on a flight to Taipei, though, so wouldn't you know I ended up on a flight to Hawaii.

I was not prepared for what happened when I got off the plane in Honolulu. Hawaii was where all the married guys went to meet up with their spouses. As we headed for the terminal, a stream of young women came running toward us with smiles and arms out-stretched. I briefly, very briefly, wondered if one of them was running toward me!

Hawaii was really relaxing. I got a small motel room off Waikiki

21. Rest and Relaxation

beach and spent most of my days in the water lying on a surfboard floating in the waves. I had a deep tan already from my time in the Nam so I did not have an issue with sunburn. I also rented a two-seater sports car and drove around the perimeter of the island and visited many of the beaches.

October 8, 1968

Dear Mom and Dad,

Well I am back over here again; it wasn't quite as hard to come back as I thought it would be. It was really great in Hawaii but all good things must come to an end. I really enjoyed lying around on the beach and surfing.

I really hope you are happy about my plans to get married it would mean a lot to me to know you are, especially dad because I know he wasn't happy about the way we got engaged.

On October 8, Alpha Company conducted an airmobile assault to establish and secure a night location site and on October 9, Alpha and Bravo companies moved into position. Over the course of the next two weeks Alpha Company conducted a reconnaissance in force missions, providing night location security and acting as ready reaction force (RRF) for the rest of the battalion.

October 19, 1968

Dear Mom and Dad,

There isn't much changed since my last letter we are still very busy and there is a rumor we are going up to the Cambodian border soon but I don't listen to rumors anymore.

October 21, 1968

Dear Mom and Dad,

I guess I am going to be a platoon sergeant at least until we get an e-6 staff sergeant in the platoon. We have three e-5 sergeants now but they decided to make me platoon sergeant and just have them be squad leaders, actually it was a big change for me but I am getting used to it. I had been a squad leader a few times on and off before I went on leave and when I came back they handed me a map and compass and said you're a platoon sergeant and you have a patrol to take out tonight. I was kind of worried the first night because I really didn't know if I could handle the job I was afraid I might make a bad decision and those are costly over here. Well anyway I have been doing all right and I kind of like having some responsibility it keeps my mind occupied because I have to know exactly where we are and make decisions I didn't have to before. It is a kind of funny situation because I am in charge of three sergeants and I am only a Specialist 4th class which is one rank below them but I don't have any problem with that. About me being put in for Sergeant I found out I am being put in at the end of the month because that is when all the promotions go in. So would you believe I will be writing up my own promotion papers because that is one of the platoon sergeant's jobs. I write up all the guys I think should be promoted and I have the Lieutenant sign it.

I have got an RTO that's a radioman from Missouri he has been here about 5 months and we get along good.

Sergeant Omboy, who was the platoon sergeant for the third platoon, rotated home around the time I went to Hawaii on leave in October. While he was in the process of leaving, he and Lt. Parr, who was by then the company CO (commanding officer), decided that I should take over as platoon sergeant. It was more than a little unusual since I had not been a squad leader other than temporarily, and I was still a Spec. 4. We also had several E5s in the platoon. They had attended the non-commissioned officer school in the states and arrived in-country as sergeants. One of them had been in-country for a few months and seemed to have gained good experience. In any case, Sergeant Omboy was insistent, and the platoon leader and CO agreed. So, in the next round of promotions I recommended myself for E5 and got the promotion.

Shortly after I got the platoon sergeant job the company was choppered (taken by helicopter) into a new location north of Saigon and close to the Cambodian border. We landed and set up a forward base camp. After just a few days we all agreed something just didn't feel right, there was something eerie about the place. None of us could put our finger on what it was that made us feel that way, but we were all uncomfortable.

There were around forty guys in my platoon, divided into four squads, ten men each. I was now the one making the decisions on

21. Rest and Relaxation

who went on patrols and ambushes, and I had to make sure they took the correct routes for patrols and got to the correct locations for ambushes. I wished I had paid better attention to map reading in basic and advance training because map reading was now a critical part of my job. I learned fast, though. I mastered the map and the responsibilities of being a platoon sergeant. I felt good about the job I was doing.

One afternoon, I told the first squad they had ambush duty that night. The squad leader was new to the role. He was tall with red hair and we called him Red. He hadn't been in-country long. The guys in his squad had been in-country longer, had seen more action, and were all close friends. They were wary of Red because they hadn't gotten to really know him yet.

Red told the squad to saddle up just after dark. Nobody moved. The squad members said they were not going out. Red came to me. I had never seen or heard of this before. I went over to the squad and they said they were not going. There was something about the place that had them on edge and they said they were not going on any more ambush patrols.

I said we had to go out, and I would go out with them. For some reason they trusted me and agreed to go. Maybe that wasn't fair to Red but I needed to solve the immediate problem. The atmosphere was really intense, so eerie, like we were being watched every step we took. We reached the ambush location and set up, and the night was uneventful. At dawn we returned to the forward base camp.

We stayed in this forward base camp for about three weeks and the uncomfortable feeling stayed with us the whole time. Then the company received new orders. Choppers would be picking up us up and taking us to a new location. However, part of my platoon was ordered to stay behind to provide security for the extraction. This was unusual for our company and our battalion since in the past when the company moved location, we all left at the same time on a single wave of choppers and we never left behind troops to provide security. I was a little confused by the orders, but orders are orders. I stayed behind along with my RTO and a squad from the platoon.

After we broke camp and the choppers left with the rest of the company my group stayed in position. Even though we had been on edge the whole time we were there, since we were on the way out, we weren't on high alert. We would only be there about thirty minutes until choppers came back to extract us. We set up in a few positions around the perimeter and waited.

As I was walking the perimeter, I saw a guy about twenty-five meters outside the perimeter yelling into the ground. He had on a military uniform and appeared to be Vietnamese. The first thing that crossed my mind was that he must be one of our Kit Carson scouts and had been left behind somehow.[1] I faced him and yelled "Hey."

The guy froze. He turned and looked at me, then did an about face and started running into the brush. The brush outside the perimeter was about three to four feet high and fairly dense, though not so dense that it would inhibit walking or running. As he started to run, I flipped the switch on my M-16 to automatic, raised it and fired off an entire magazine. I missed. I could still see his silhouette through the brush. I quickly grabbed another magazine and reloaded. I flipped the switch to semi-automatic, took aim and fired. The guy fell down. I told the platoon I thought he was NVA and that we might be sitting on an NVA bunker system. Privately, I was shocked the NVA were not already out of their holes since there were so few of us still there, but they probably thought the entire company was still with us.

I asked one of the guys to follow me and we headed out into the brush to see if we could find the NVA soldier. We couldn't know if he was wounded or killed but we had to assume he was wounded and would put up a fight. We were also nervous that the other NVA would come out of the tunnels and attack us. But I thought we needed to know what was going on. As we approached the NVA soldier, we heard an explosion. The NVA soldier had detonated a hand grenade under his body. He was an NVA officer armed with a nine-millimeter pistol. By the time we reached him he was dead.

We made our way back to the platoon. I grabbed the receiver from my RTO and called back the CO. I told him about the NVA officer who was yelling into a hole and that the NVA were right there under our feet. I asked him to send back the company and told him we might

21. Rest and Relaxation

need the full battalion. The CO responded that we had our orders, and the choppers would be back to extract us.

I was in shock. How could that be? We were going to leave a place where it was fairly certain we had NVA bunker under our feet and we had the advantage. Instead, we were going to head out to another landing zone that could be a hot landing zone in search of NVA where they would likely have the ambush advantage.

The CO said it was an order. We were to protect the perimeter and be prepared for extraction. We set up and watched for any movement from outside the perimeter and waited for the choppers. When they arrived about fifteen minutes later, we jumped on and off we went. Not a single NVA appeared. They had to be there. There was no way an NVA officer was out there alone yelling into the ground. I think the NVA officer thought we had all pulled out, not realizing part of a platoon had been left behind for security.

Some days later we were on patrol somewhere north of Tay Ninh when we got word that we would be picked up by helicopters and brought back to Tay Ninh to meet with the battalion commander to be briefed on an assault of a newly discovered NVA base camp. The choppers arrived and the company loaded. We arrived at the airfield in Tay Ninh and were told to have leadership get off the choppers to meet with the battalion commander for the briefing. That meant the company commander, platoon leaders, and platoon sergeants. I was a platoon sergeant at the time, so I got off the chopper and went with the others to the briefing. We each had an RTO assigned to us and all of the RTOs got off the choppers as well and stayed close by the leadership team.

I didn't pay attention at the time, but I was the only one who took my M-16 with me to the meeting. Everyone else left their M-16s on the choppers. One or two of the officers may have had .45 caliber pistols with them but most likely not, since they usually carried M-16s or M-15s (like an M-16 but shorter) instead.

The choppers sat on the airfield with the engines running while we met with the colonel. The colonel provided us with details about the NVA base camp we were going to attack, and instructions on how the assault was to be conducted. The choppers would touch down in a landing zone just outside what Command believed was the NVA base camp perimeter. We would then assault that perimeter and engage the enemy. The size of the NVA troop strength was not known but if we needed reinforcements choppers would bring in other companies from the battalion.

As the colonel was finishing his instructions to us, the choppers carrying our troops began lifting off and leaving the airfield without us. One of the guys in my platoon had been left behind as well. He must have stepped off the chopper for some reason before they took off and he had his M-16 with him.

The colonel got on the radio and contacted the headquarters of the helicopter unit to try to find out what was going on and to get them to bring the choppers back. The colonel was yelling at whomever he was talking to. We never found out why they left without us. When the choppers came back about thirty minutes later, they were empty, and the pilots said they dropped our troops off at the landing zone.

We were all frustrated but also worried, so we jumped into the choppers and the company commander gave the pilots the landing zone coordinates and told the pilots to take us there. I am not sure why he didn't just say "take us to our troops" but he didn't. It turned out the company commander had the correct coordinates but that was not where the choppers had dropped the rest of our men. They had been dropped miles away from the actual landing zone in a field with no radios and they were waiting for orders. For some reason the pilot just followed the company commander's orders about where to take the leadership team and never said anything, like, "okay but that is not where we took your men."

As we approached the correct landing zone in the choppers we started taking fire from a large contingent of NVA from bunkers in a wood line to our left. In the confusion we assumed our troops were on the ground engaging the enemy. We ordered the choppers into the landing zone. As we landed the firing continued. We hit the

21. Rest and Relaxation

ground and spread out to find our men so we could coordinate an attack.

Pretty quickly we figured out that our men weren't there. The entire leadership team was on the ground taking fire from what we later learned may have been a battalion of NVA who were dug in and firing from bunkers. None of our men were there and only two of us had anything more than a .45 caliber pistol. That was me and the guy in my platoon who had been left behind.

I knew it wouldn't be long before the NVA realized that only a small group of us had landed and no others were coming, and as soon as they realized that they would mount an attack instead of firing from their bunkers. "What should we do?" the platoon leader asked me. "We should get the hell out of here as fast as we can."

The landing zone was actually a large swamp. The NVA base camp was in a dry wood line and we were in the swamp about fifty yards from the wood line. That distance gave us a chance to escape. The swamp had grasses that stood two to three feet high in most places, giving us some cover but not much given the NVA knew exactly where we landed.

I turned away from the wood line and started moving (running but hindered by the swamp) as fast as I could. My platoon leader (I don't recall his name) and everyone else followed. We stayed as low as we could while running. The firing was intense. The only advantage we had was the NVA would never think that we'd attack with such a small group of men, so they'd have to assume that there were more troops on the way, or maybe they thought we were bringing in Cobra gunships. If they figured out what was really going on, they would have been out of their bunkers in no time coming after us.

We ran for about thirty minutes then slowed to a walk when the firing stopped, and we felt like we were far enough away. We were safe for the moment. However, we were also not far from a large NVA unit that knew exactly where we were.

We radioed back for an extraction. By then, the colonel had figured out what happened. He sent the chopper unit back to find us. We were picked up and brought to the field where our troops were waiting, miles away. They were lounging around, confused and waiting for orders. We called in for new orders. We were told to get back on the choppers and go back to our original position, where we started the day, and not to where we knew there was an NVA unit.

I have no idea what went on at battalion headquarters that day. We spend day after day looking for NVA, then we find them, screw up the assault beyond comprehension, and then leave and go look for them someplace else, instead of regrouping and going back to where we know they are. Maybe Command sent in artillery or called an air strike after we left. Maybe by the time things got sorted out they had intelligence that the NVA had withdrawn from the area. I don't know and will never understand some of the decisions that were made.

October 22, 1968
Dear Mom and Dad,

I just received two letters from each of you. It was really great to hear from you I have been waiting for a letter but now I understand how it is with Grandma. I am really hoping she will be all right, I am going to write her again and give her strict orders to get well. Grandma has a lot of will power and I believe she will pull through and will be home when I get there, then I can kid around with her again.

It was really a shock to hear about Herb Burnside but it is easy to believe with the way he has been the last few years. It must be a terrible thing for his mother, she never really knew what to do with him especially after he started on that stuff.

A few weeks ago Wagner got a letter from home saying an old friend of his was killed in an accident and he was saying how he couldn't get over it him being over here and doing alright and one of his friends gets it back home, now I know what he meant. I kind of wish I could have gone to the funeral and talk to Herb's mother for a minute.

I don't know what to say about what you said about my award and the newspaper clipping, this is one of those things that I am at a loss of words about. I will say I am glad you are proud of me, that makes me feel good.

I am in Cu Chi now that is the base camp I was in when I had bad feet back in April. The company was sent in for two days of rest. Tonight we are having steaks and beer and soda because it is our first night in. I hope no one gets offended if I don't write much until things slow down.

21. Rest and Relaxation

November 1, 1968

Dear Mom and Dad,

I have a few minutes before our resupply comes in and we move out again. I am really sorry I forgot your birthday Mom I just have so many things to think about lately that I can't keep track of what is going on at home. About sending me something for Christmas the best Christmas present you could give me a box full of those chocolate chip cookies Kris made a few times. I really can't use anything else.

Chapter 22

Bereavement Leave

During October and the early part of November we were mostly north of Saigon in the same area of the Ho Mon bridge and Go Vap. We moved between there and the area around and north of Tay Ninh toward the Cambodian border. We engaged in numerous search and destroy patrols, ambush patrols and chopper assaults. I was feeling good about what I was doing as platoon sergeant and my experience in-country. The contact with Charlie occurred but not with the intensity of my early months in the Nam. On the other hand, things seemed sort of dark to me especially when around the border. I could not put my finger on what it was. I had a feeling that bad things were coming in terms of engagement with Charlie.

The officers seemed to rotate every few months. Before long the lieutenant in my platoon rotated off the line to a rear area job and was replaced. Sometime after he was back in the World, he went to my parents' house looking for me. He told my parents I had saved his life. I wish I could remember his name and what he meant about saving his life.

By now, Lt. Parr was the company CO. He told me he wanted me to attend leadership school. It was the Reconnaissance and Surveillance Leaders Course, a three-week course to be conducted in Vietnam in the near future. Lt. Parr had the credentials and contacts to make it happen and I was interested. I think he was also concerned that a more senior NCO would be assigned to our platoon and he would be pressured to move me to squad leader and let the higher-ranking NCO take over my role as platoon sergeant. The training would allow him to

22. Bereavement Leave

put me up for staff sergeant (E6) as well as give me additional skills for the platoon sergeant job. The leadership course was scheduled to begin in mid–November.

Sure enough, in the beginning of November a sergeant first class (E7) was assigned to our company and to the third platoon. He and I functioned as joint platoon sergeants initially, and the plan was to continue that way until I left for the leadership school. They would decide when I got back what to do with me in terms of what platoon I would be assigned to.

November 5, 1968
Dear Mom and Dad,

We are pulling road security for a convoy that will be coming through so I borrowed a sheet of paper and write a few words while I am sitting here. I haven't had any time to write the last few days. We are still on the go all the time they should give us a little time off soon, most of the guys are so tired they can't stay awake on guard and most of the time too tired to eat. I should have most of tomorrow off. We got a new lieutenant yesterday but I haven't decided whether I like him as much as the last one, our old lieutenant got another job off the line he really wasn't suited for this anyway but we got along good. Well there isn't much to say except I hope Grandma is doing all right now.

We got a Sergeant first class (e-7) in the platoon and he will be taking over as Platoon Sergeant as soon as he gets the hang of things. He has been here a few days, we get along pretty good. He should take over in a few days and I will be assistant Platoon Sergeant until I go to leadership school in a few weeks. The Platoon Lieutenant is sending me to leadership school and said I would probably be a Platoon Sergeant of another platoon when I get back but I said I wanted to stay with the third platoon so he said he would try to have me come back as a squad leader if that is what I wanted and I agreed. The school is nine days, one thing I like about it, it will be a little rest.

I have been here for 8 months and one day and I have 120 !!! days left, that doesn't sound too long compared to 365 when I first got here.

On November 12, my grandmother died. I know she was praying for me all the time. I know everyone worried about me, but my grandmother lost her son in World War II, so I think she worried the most. When someone in your immediate family dies, you are allowed to go home for the funeral. Since my grandmother lived with us in our house, she was considered part of my immediate family, so they came out in the field to let me know I could go home for the funeral.

We were getting ready to head out on a search and destroy when I was called to the command post. There was chopper leaving soon that would take me to Tay Ninh to start my journey home. I guess it should have been an easy decision to get on the chopper and go. The decision was not easy for me. So many things ran through my mind. I knew my parents would want me to come home, but I would be leaving all my friends in the platoon and the company. So many thoughts were running through my mind. "I am getting used to this and I can handle it." "What if I go home and come back and I can't handle it?" "What if my platoon hits some heavy fighting while I am gone, and I am not there to help?"

I was the platoon sergeant at that point and I was worried that I shouldn't leave my unit. I also wasn't sure I could ever come back if I left. I had three minutes to decide; the chopper was waiting. We were at a forward fire support base getting ready to go out on patrol. I said no at first, and then quickly changed my mind.

I have this strange thing about letting things take their course, sort of like the natural order of things. Things happen for a reason. Maybe I was meant to leave, to go home now. And we had the new E7 to take over the platoon. I decided to go. I told Lt. Parr and the new platoon sergeant and said a few quick good-byes and jumped on the chopper. Lt. Parr had taken over as the company commander and the third platoon got a new platoon leader, Lt. Hudson, I believe. I didn't really have a chance to get to know the new platoon leader before I left. As we lifted off I had so many emotions. I felt like I was leaving my guys.

I made my way from Tay Ninh to Saigon by catching a military transport to Ton Sun Nhut air base and waited for a freedom bird to take me home. The freedom bird was full of guys who had completed their tours, who wouldn't be coming back. I didn't belong on this plane. I couldn't imagine what it would be like to be back in the states. I didn't know if emotionally I could get on a plane to come back to Vietnam. And my grandma just died. It was all very hard, and very surreal.

22. Bereavement Leave

I finally arrived home about five days later. Upon arrival in the U.S., I realized that, at 20 years old, I was not old enough to drink alcohol in Connecticut and most states. It was not a big deal for me but seemed strange given what I had been through over the past eight months. I had a seven-day leave, so I wouldn't have to go back until after thanksgiving. I missed my grandmother's funeral of course, but it was good to be home and see my family and friends. A few of my friends spent one drunken evening trying to break my arm so I would not have to go back. Once I was home, I would have been happy to stay. In hindsight, I probably could have tried to get my orders changed. I just didn't think of that at that time.

After my week leave was up, my parents drove me to JFK for a flight to Oakland, California. I noticed my father tearing up while I getting ready to board. I think he was feeling like I was. Going back was much harder. Now I knew what I was going back to, and so did my dad.

When I arrived in Oakland, I made my way to the Army terminal and went to check in. The guy at the desk said I was late. He said I was supposed to have reported back in seven days. "What the hell are you talking about?" I asked.

"You are supposed to be in Vietnam already. You had seven days to get home and get back." The person on the other side of the desk didn't seem to care much about anything, and clearly didn't understand that it took just about that long to get home in the first place.

"I didn't know that. They said I had seven days. I thought they meant seven days at home." "Well too bad, we aren't paying your way back."

There was a long pause while I was weighing all my options. "Okay, I won't go back then" I replied. "Okay, then you will be AWOL and we will come and arrest you and you will go to prison."

Another fairly long pause. "Well, what am I supposed to do then？" "I will give you an advance on your pay. Go to the San Francisco airport and buy a ticket."

He gave me the money and I got on a bus and went to the San Francisco airport. I walked around the airport until I found an airline that had flights to Vietnam (why anyone would voluntarily fly to

Vietnam Stories I Never Told

Vietnam then I had no idea). I bought a ticket for a flight leaving 36 hours later. The plane ticket cost $250. That does not sound like much but it was equivalent to several months' pay. The Army deducted some money out of my pay each month until it was repaid.

While I was waiting around for the flight, I fell asleep. An MP (military policeman) woke me up and told me to get up and walk around. He said I was acting "unmilitary." I was so happy to board the plane later, just so I could sleep.

A couple of days after leaving New York I landed in Saigon. I went to the military counter at the airport and asked where my unit was. They didn't know, and didn't offer any assistance or have any ideas on what I should do next. Since my unit had been near Tay Ninh when I left, I figured going there was my best option. I hung around the hangers until I found a plane headed to Tay Ninh.

When I arrived in Tay Ninh I went to the command. Nobody I talked to knew where my unit was either. I got on a plane back to Saigon and then got on a flight to Cu Chi, thinking my unit might be there. When I got to Cu Chi, they told me my unit had moved to Dau Tieng, so I flew back to Saigon, and waited for a flight to Dau Tieng.

December 14, 1968

Dear Mom and Dad,

I am in Saigon now, which is Saturday and will be catching a flight to Dau Tieng in the morning I am doing okay and am feeling alright except for being a little lonesome. The flight took 20 hours, we stopped at Hawaii, Guam and Manila and I sat next to a girl who was coming over here to marry a construction worker, I think she has a loose wire someplace to come here to get married.

Dau Tieng Base Camp was twenty-four kilometers east of Tay Ninh. The Third Brigade of the Twenty-Fifth Infantry Division was stationed there at the time. When I arrived, I learned my unit was out in the field, but at least I was in the right place. The first person I saw was the company first sergeant. "What the hell are you doing here?"

"I came back." "Nobody comes back." I must be the only person in the world crazy enough to come back, and pay my own way back, into this war.

22. Bereavement Leave

I still had on my winter dress uniform and it was easily 100 degrees and I had been traveling in that uniform for about a week. They gave me fatigues, an M-16, and the next day I got on a helicopter and there I was, back running around the rice paddies and getting shot at again.

When I got back to my unit, I found out that on Thanksgiving Day, while I was still at home in the states, Alpha Company and Bravo Company, along with Alpha Company Second Battalion, Twenty-Second Infantry Regiment encountered an enemy battalion three miles south of Tay Ninh City. Lt. Parr was killed that day, along with 18 other guys in my company, and 36 men in my company were wounded. Even today, I still wonder if I did the right thing, leaving Vietnam to go home when I did.

Going back to Vietnam was probably the hardest thing I have ever done in my life. And not just because the Army made it just about impossible for me to get there. I felt like I was looking death in the face. When I got back I knew what was ahead of me and that is so much harder than going in green. My closest friends were back home. Davis was wounded earlier in the year while in recon and sent to a hospital in the states. Saylor and Wagner had both been wounded and were home recovering as well. Wagner had been wounded the day after I left the field for home. Lt. Parr was dead. I felt completely alone.

All of those I knew who were killed had a lasting effect on me but none more than Lt. Parr. We bonded really quickly. I looked out for him and he did the same for me. I was shocked that a West Pointer could take such an interest in me. And I was really impressed by his sense of duty and country. I still feel the guilt for not being there that Thanksgiving Day.

When I got back to my unit that day, I also found out that on December 2, while I was on my way back to Vietnam I was officially promoted to sergeant.

Vietnam Stories I Never Told

December 16, 1968

Dear Mom and Dad,

I got back to my company today and they told me I had enough mail and packages for three men to carry. I got a letter from Davis, he is alright and just got back from a sick leave and is waiting to be reassigned. He is still at the hospital until he gets reassignment orders. He said he still has some metal in his chest but they are going to leave it there.

While I was gone things weren't too good, they lost about one third of the company. Wagner got hit by a bobby trap that someone else set off and he got a broken jaw and two broken legs he is back in the states in a hospital. The guys said he took it calmer than anybody they had seen. He asked for a drink of water and rinsed his mouth, spit out about three teeth and said "man it feels good to get them out"

Well there's not much more to say except from now on you can call me Sergeant, well maybe since you're my family I will let you call me Herb. I got my orders today.

On December 18, Alpha Company was operating out of the Dau Tieng base camp. Bravo and Charlie companies joined engineers of Alpha Company, 65th Engineers and built a forward base camp called Mole City in literally one day. There were bunkers on the perimeter, similar to a rear area base camp, that were about eight feet tall and ten feet square with wooden bunks for eight men and a thick wooden wall between the firing location in front and the sleeping area in the rear. There were sandbags on the sides and top. The firing location was about three feet wide and had openings for sight and firing. Each bunker had a squad assigned to it. Mole City was around nine miles south of Tay Ninh, in a VC infested area that had not been patrolled by U.S. forces for more than a year. It was also located along one of the most used infiltration routes used by the NVA reentering Vietnam from Cambodia.

December 20, 1968

Dear Mom and Dad,

I am out in the field again, I am a squad leader in my old platoon but it isn't bad because we don't go out much. We are between Tay Ninh and the Cambodian border. I have a feeling I will be getting off the line soon maybe in about 20 days.

I am driving the guys crazy talking about how good it was to be back in the

22. Bereavement Leave

states as a matter of fact I am going to have to stop talking about it because I am making myself homesick.

On December 22, Alpha Company was still operating out of Dau Tieng. We were out in the field most of the time. Being out in the field is usually the worst place to be, but that was not the case on December 22.

In the early morning hours of December 22, the NVA launched a massive ground assault on Mole City. At the time Bravo, Charlie and Echo companies were protecting the base. The attack began with fierce mortar, seventy-five-millimeter recoilless rifles and RPGs, immediately followed by small arms and automatic weapons fire. The battle continued for seven hours, and the NVA were able to penetrate the trench line between two of the Mole City bunkers. The Manchus' response was massive. The volume of fire was so heavy that four M-60 machine gun barrels melted. Seventeen guys in Bravo, Charlie and Echo were killed and thirty-four were wounded.

Alpha Company was sent to the French Fort later that day or the next. The French Fort was, not surprisingly, built by the French, and later reinforced by the Army Corp of Engineers. The fort had large bunkers made of four-by-fours and plywood covered by sandbags. The bunkers were built into a berm that had been created. They had a front room with firing portholes and that room had a wall that separated it from the sleeping area that slept six on wooden bunks. My recollection is you could stand up straight in the bunkers so they must have been over six-feet high inside, making them more like eight feet high outside.

Most of us took our turns on guard duty sitting on top of the bunker, which afforded a great view of the low brush area in front to the tree lines further out. The camp had a mess hooch and latrines and the big artillery guns in the center that were used to fire artillery rounds into Cambodia. The big guns fired all night every night. I think the guns were 175mm, or maybe the M110, howitzers that fired eight-inch self-propelled rounds. The bunkers were stuffy inside so I tried sleeping outside a few times. That was a failed strategy because

I felt like I was being lifted off the ground every time one of the big guns fired.

We ran sweeps out of the camp to ensure the NVA were not digging in outside the perimeter. We ran some nightly ambush patrols. We guarded the base camp and the guns. My heart really wasn't into this anymore. I no longer had the sort of bravado that I had before I went home. I didn't mind being a squad leader but I didn't like it as much as being the platoon sergeant. Leadership school was off the table unless I extended my tour. The Army had a deal where you could extend for two months and then muster out at the end of the tour rather than getting reassigned to a unit in the states. Sergeant Hale wanted me to extend and he said he would get me promoted to staff sergeant if I did.

December 25, 1968
Dear Mom and Dad,

It is Christmas and we have the day off today so I am catching up on writing. I heard my company is supposed to go into Tay Ninh for a couple of weeks and then we will be moving someplace else it's all rumors so I won't believe it until it happens. I hope you are having a good Christmas, you know this is the second Christmas I haven't been home. Well next year Sherri and I will come over for Christmas.

The next night I was sitting on top of the bunker on my guard rotation. The night was clear and warm, and quiet. Around midnight I heard a shot from the bunker next to me. Then another shot. Then another. Pretty soon the bunker was popping like a popcorn maker. There was no fire coming from the perimeter or beyond, so I knew we were not under attack. The guys in the bunker were in my platoon and most of them smoked marijuana regularly. They also had a habit of having candles burning in the bunker while they enjoyed the grass. At first, I thought they were shooting at each other, but quickly realized they must have fallen asleep with the candles burning and somehow the bunker caught on fire.

Each bunker was fully stocked with M-16 and M-60 rounds as well as M-72 LAWS[1] and M-90 ammunition rounds and grenades. These rounds of ammunition are highly explosive. I could see the

22. Bereavement Leave

entrance of the bunker. No one came out. I wondered if they were all dead. I jumped down from my perch and ran to the entrance, got on my stomach and crawled in. Most of the firing was actually in the front area, not in the back by the bunks where the guys were. The bunker was also on fire and the smoke was starting to get thick so it was hard to see. I think the guys in there were dazed and it hadn't registered yet what was happening. I yelled to them and grabbed feet and pulled them toward the door. The other guys followed, and we all crawled out and away from the bunker.

We stood outside watching as the flames engulfed the bunker and smoke poured out. The firefight going on inside continued. Then there was a huge explosion that actually lifted the top off the bunker off the sandbags. The explosion knocked those of us near the bunker to the ground and one guy who was on top of my bunker got knocked off and landed on us. There were some minor burns but no major injuries.

The CO was all over the squad from the bunker, questioning them about what had happened. No one would say. The platoon sergeant had seen me go in but he never mentioned it to CO. I think he stayed silent because he did not want me to have to answer any questions. The next day the CO ordered the squad to rebuild the bunker by hand. That was no easy task.

December 27, 1968
Dear Mom and Dad,

We are still in the same camp. Last night one of the bunkers caught on fire with all explosives and ammo in it and it was like the fourth of July around here. It was the bunker next to mine and when the whole bunker blew finally it knocked about 5 of us over and we were on the other side of our bunker all I could see was flaming metal and wood in the air. Some guys were burned but when I hit the ground another guy was knocked off the bunker and landed on top of me and shielded me from it.

One of the guys wrote to Wagner's home to find out where he is and how he is doing and he got a letter back saying Wagner was in the hospital in the states and that he would be home for Christmas.

Time continued and with each day and on each patrol, I became more careful. I knew more than I did when I arrived in-country so I knew

Vietnam Stories I Never Told

what to look for and where not to go and how to avoid paths and take routes that were less likely to lead us directly into an ambush. But there was a problem. I was thinking about going home and that I might actually make it. That's why the Army takes short-timers off the line if they can.

December 31, 1968

Dear Mom and Dad,

I really haven't been doing much lately because we don't go out on sweeps very often and when they have details all I have to do is get the men there and put one of my team leaders in charge. I spent part of the morning explaining a few things to a new guy in my squad and getting him set up. Now the rest of the squad is on a detail filling sandbags for a new bunker and I have been sitting here reading a book most of the afternoon. I have got nine men in my squad now and we are at full strength now, each platoon has 30 men they have really built up since I got back about half my platoon is new men.

One of the guys got a letter from Wagner. He said he is doing okay, he has the cast off one leg already and a walking cast on the other leg and he has his mouth wired shut so his jaw will heal. He asked in the letter if I was back over here or not so I wrote to him and sent it to the hospital. I sent him a letter to the hospital he was supposed to be in in Japan but I guess he left before it got there. You know I left the field the evening of Nov 14 and Wagner got hit the next morning. Remember the lieutenant I used to talk about named Parr (I was his radio man when he first got here) well he was killed while I was home. I didn't mention it because I didn't feel like talking about it. We were pretty good friends but I was always worried about him because he thought he was invincible.

The reason we don't have too many sweeps here is because this is what they call a fire support base, we have artillery here and we just pull security for them and they support the troops on the Cambodian border. This is a permanent outpost that is why it is built up so good.

January 6, 1969

Dear Mom and Dad,

We are supposed to move in the next few days. I haven't gotten the word on where we are going but it is supposed to be around Tay Ninh and we aren't far from Tay Ninh now. I am going to mark where I think we are going on the map at the bottom of the page. It is really getting hot over here now and everything is turning to dust but I still like it better than all that rain and mud.

22. Bereavement Leave

The medic just came over and handed out our malaria pills we take once a week and I just thought of something I probably never told you. Over here there is only two ways we know what day of the week it is and they are— whenever there is messed up music on the radio we know it is Sunday and whenever we get malaria pills it is Monday. Well that is all for now, see you in "62" days.

January 10, 1969

Dear Mom and Dad,

We were supposed to leave this base camp today or tomorrow and clear the road for the engineers to go to Tay Ninh, then we were supposed to stay in Tay Ninh for a few days and move someplace else but we can't go because they can't get another company in to secure this base camp. Nobody seems to know how long it will be now before we leave here but I guess I don't mind staying here even though it's boring because when we go someplace else I may wish I was back here getting bored again. They have been a lot better about getting clean clothes out to us than they used to, we got a new colonel and he says we should have clean clothes twice a week and they have been doing that ever since we got back.

January 16, 1969

Dear Mom and Dad,

We were up almost all-night last night and I am kind of tired but I realized I hadn't written in a few days so I figured I better write and let you know I am doing alright.

There is something I think I should tell you before you start to get worried since I came back over here I feel like I am going through a lot of changes and I just don't have it in me to write as often as I used to. It's not that I am depressed or anything like that in fact leaving home this time was easier than any other time since I left to be drafted. I am getting used to being away from home now and I am getting used to being away for a while and going home for a few short weeks and leaving again. So if you don't get as many letters don't worry about it.

Leaving home, coming back to Vietnam wasn't easier, not at all. I just didn't want them to worry.

Chapter 23

Short Timer

One day the first sergeant came out to the camp and called me aside. He said he would like to know if I wanted to extend and if so, we could discuss what that would mean. I told him I had thought about it but had decided not to extend. He then thanked me for all I had done during my tour and said he would like me to move off the line to the company headquarters group and run re-supply for the balance of my tour. That meant I would give up my squad leader job and move to the company headquarters bunker in the center of the perimeter and order and take delivery of supplies as well as the occasional trip back the rear area headquarters location in Tay Ninh.

I really like Top (the first sergeant). He had always been a real professional and I liked the idea of working for him for the balance of my tour. It wasn't really optional, even so I said thanks, and I told him I liked the idea. I had made one new friend in my time back with the platoon. I guess two if you count the platoon sergeant who was also a real professional. The other was the guy who had been my RTO before I left and was still the RTO for the platoon sergeant. He was from Missouri and had a deep drawl. I worried about him and the other platoon members, but it was time to move on and, unless I could change how I was feeling, I was not sure I was at my best anyway.

January 20, 1969
Dear Mom and Dad,

Well I have some good news for a change. I have been taken off the line and I am now in charge of resupply in the field. The first Sergeant is going home on leave in two days and I had my doubts if he was going to take me

23. Short Timer

off before he left but he came out to the field yesterday and told me to pack up my things and move up to the resupply bunker. The Sergeant in charge of resupply is leaving in a few days so I am taking over. In a way I felt bad about leaving the platoon but I figure it is time for me to stop messing around on the line and take it easy for the rest of my tour. The first Sergeant told me he thought I have done an outstanding job on the line and it was time for me to take it easy for awhile. About three days ago I was at a squad leader meeting and our platoon leader was trying to talk me into extending over here and staying in the platoon he said he would have me promoted to staff Sergeant if I would extend. I told him I felt I had been over here long enough and I wanted to leave at my regular date. I was talking to the battalion P.I.O. man (he takes pictures and writes news stories) and he said he had been talking to the LT and he had told him he would rather have me in the field with him than any other NCO in the company. This LT was our platoon leader for about two weeks before I went home and Sergeant Hale became Platoon Sergeant a few days before I left so I worked with the LT for awhile and gave him advice and we got along good. 49 days left.

P.S. *This resupply job I stay out at the forward base most of the time but I never go on patrol.*

January 23, 1969

Dear Mom and Dad,

Well I am enjoying taking it easy for a change. I have enough to do to keep me busy part of the day and then I have time to relax. I am so used to pulling guard duty for a few hours every night that now I wake up in the middle of the night and can't sleep for awhile. We have a big bunker that we live in with lights and a fan in it so I have it just as good out here as I would in Tay Ninh.

January 29, 1969

Dear Mom and Dad,

I have been busy all morning counting up all the ammunition we have out here and making a report on it. We are supposed to have a half a million rounds of M16 ammo and the same amount for machine guns and we have about half that much so I have to keep ordering some every day until we have it. I have two big bunkers so full of ammo I can hardly move in them and that's only half of what we are supposed to have out here I think we could hold off a division with all this ammo. I have a jeep and driver to take me around whenever I go to Tay Ninh. I have it pretty good now but I still can't wait to go home. This war will be over for me and I will only have about 6 and a half months left to serve. I'm glad I went into the army when I *did because it won't be long and I will be out and won't have to worry about being drafted like a lot of guys my age. Even though I don't really like the service life I don't really regret the time I have put in because it has taught me a lot about myself and other people and also how to handle people. Well I have 41 days left now and I can't wait until they are over. I still haven't gotten my reassignment orders.*

February 5, 1969
Dear Mom and Dad,
   I got a letter from my old friend Davis today, I think he is kind of hoping I will be reassigned at Fort Hood with him, it is kind of far from Stamford but we would have a good time if I went there. He said that it was a mighty lucky gook to get him and get away with it, he was only kidding but that was the way he was he never thought about getting hit and it never worried him, I didn't think he would ever get hit either.

On one of my trips to the rear area, TOP got the headquarters group together and presented me with a Bronze Star. I asked him what it was for and he said for a year of outstanding service with the company. He also told everyone that I was the highest decorated soldier in the company at that time. Maybe the Bronze Star was in place of the second Silver Star I was recommended for the day Sergeant Hiebert was killed. TOP did not say and I did not ask him.

February 7, 1969 Award of the Bronze Star signed, for service March 1968 to March 1969. Citation By Direction of the president The Bronze Star Metal is presented to Sergeant Herbert G. Jansen who distinguished himself by outstandingly meritorious service in connection with military operations against a hostile force in the Republic of Vietnam. During the period March 1968 to March 1969, he consistently manifested exemplary professionalism and initiative in obtaining outstanding results. His rapid assessment and solution of numerous problems inherent in a combat environment greatly enhanced the allied effectiveness against a determined and aggressive enemy. Despite many adversities, he invariably performed his duties in a resolute and efficient manner. Energetically applying his sound judgment and extensive knowledge, he has contributed materially to the successful accomplishment of the United States in the Republic of Vietnam. His loyalty, diligence and devotion to duty were in keeping with the highest traditions of the military service and reflect great credit upon himself and the United States Army.

23. Short Timer

February 19, 1969

Dear Mom and Dad,

  I still don't have any orders yet so I still don't know exactly when I will be home but I will leave no later than March 10 because if I don't have orders by then they will just send me to California and get reassigned from there. In about 12 days I will be going into Tay Ninh for good to start clearing post. I think I am getting what they call short time pains, a lot of guys over here when they get close to going home they start to act funny either forgetful or they get mad easy but with me all kind of things are happening. I am in a daze half the time. That's why they usually take men off line about two or three months before they go home only with me it didn't bother me until lately. Well it's time for me to go back into my daze again, I'll see you in 19 days.

February 20, 1969

Dear Mom and Dad,

  Right now the company is getting ready to go out on an eagle flight (that means they are going out on choppers and get dropped off someplace and go on a sweep) but I am just laying around taking it easy I won't have anything to do until this afternoon when our resupply comes in.

February 22, 1969 (last letter)

Dear Mom and Dad,

  I have been trying to stay as busy as possible the last few days to keep my mind busy so I won't think about going home. I've been a bundle of energy lately I never seem to get tired. Whenever the company goes out I feel like going with them but I know it wouldn't be a wise thing to do right now so I just stay here and try to stay busy.

Finally, the day came. I was leaving the field for good and heading to Saigon for the flight home. I said my good-byes in the field and the rear area and headed for the airfield at Tay Ninh. From there it was to Cu Chi and then a flight to Tan Son Nhut. I was still in my fatigues like all the others lining up for the Freedom Bird. We all looked tan and the fatigues were faded. I know we all looked happy but I also know we were all still scared, scared that somehow we still might not make it home alive.

We watched the plane land and the FNGs disembark. They walked

Vietnam Stories I Never Told

by us and starred at us. Some of the short timers yelled "short" and "FNGs," just like when I arrived here a year ago, even though I know we all felt bad for the guys just arriving. We knew what they were in for. Body bags were there, waiting to be loaded on the plane, like every other day at Tan Son Nhut.

Once on the plane we all cheered. I looked out the window and reflected on all that had occurred in the past year. I almost could not believe I was sitting there with all my limbs and no purple heart. I knew I had done the best I could and that is all that anyone can do. When we landed at Oakland, we all got rid of our fatigues and were issued new dress uniforms. I had left the Nam with nothing but the clothes on my back and that is the way I left Oakland. We got advances for our flights home and took a bus to San Francisco airport to book a flight. I landed at JFK Airport in NYC and took a bus to the Stamford CT train station, which was a few miles from my home.

When I got off the train I headed home on foot. I had been walking more than five miles a day with fifty to seventy pounds of gear just about every day for the last year. Walking a few miles to my house was nothing and I just wanted to take it all in. This day was one of the happiest days of my life.

I walked down the road alongside the tracks that led to U.S. 1 and then past my old corner hangout and deli. None of my old friends were there. They had moved on or were in the Nam or at some stateside base camp. I said hello to the deli owner and moved on past the projects where some of my old friends had lived. I finally arrived home and walked in the back door. The door entered the kitchen and, sure enough, my mother was standing in the kitchen in her housedress with an apron on. She ran to me, and we hugged. I think she had been holding her breath the whole time I was gone.

**** The End ****

Afterword

I had orders for Fort Hood, Texas, on my return to the states. I would be placed in a stateside infantry unit. I had no interest in playing army on my return so I drove to Fort Dix and asked one of the clerks how I could get my orders changed to be part of a basic training unit. He gave me the information for an office in the Pentagon that had the authority to change orders. I drove immediately to the airport and got a flight to DC and went to the Pentagon.

When I arrived in the office it was jammed with young soldiers who had orders for Vietnam and wanted to request a hardship change. When my turn came, I went in and explained what I wanted and the sergeant behind the desk smiled and said, "you got it." I left with orders for Fort Dix.

I only had six months left and worked with three basic training companies as a drill sergeant. I also was the physical training instructor for my company. It was one of the most rewarding jobs I have ever had. My first sergeant did everything he could to get me to re-enlist, including an offer to recommend me for West Point on a program that was apparently in place at that time for noncommissioned officers who had served in Vietnam. At the time I had no idea about college or what the military academy was all about and had no confidence that I would succeed.

In September 1969, I decided for sure I did not want to remain in the Army. I was discharged and returned to my old job at the telephone company. I quit several years later and attended the University of Tennessee, majoring in accounting. I joined an accounting firm after I

Afterword

finished school and obtained my CPA license. In nine years, I was promoted to partner. Over the course of my career, I consulted with Fortune 500 companies and their executives, lead a global business line with over 3,000 employees and revenues of $1 billion, and was part of the global management team of a company with 80,000 employees.

I did marry my girlfriend Sherri at the end of my military service. We were too young and the marriage did not last. Fortunately, we remain friends to this day. A few years later I married my second wife and had a son and a daughter. After twenty years of marriage, my second wife and I divorced. A few years later I married Anne and she is truly the love of my life. I guess the third time really is a charm. I now have a step-daughter too, and ten grandchildren. My children and grandchildren are my greatest accomplishments. Anne and I just celebrated our 27th wedding anniversary.

One of the things my Vietnam experience gave me is I learned how to learn. I had never been particularly good in school although that might have been due to lack of motivation. In Vietnam, although it may seem to be to the contrary, I had lots of "quiet" time to think and learn. Every night, whether in a forward base camp or on ambush patrols, we were typically set up in three-man positions. The guard rotation was one hour on and two off and one on again and so on until daybreak. I found that I had to find something besides looking for Charlie to occupy my time.

I chose things I knew something about and tried to dissect them and learn them to the point of owning them in my mind. For instance, I thought about the U.S. telephone system and how the network operated. I had some knowledge from my year working as a technician with the telephone company. I took that knowledge and created the technical links in my mind as to how each call was processed locally, nationally and internationally. That included how each digit caused a switch to activate and move the call through the system down to the power and emergency power that operated the system. As a result of this "self-training" I found that in college I never had to take notes. I could retain the lectures and then evaluate them later and take ownership of the material that way.

Afterword

I also know how lucky I am. I went to Vietnam and came home with no physical wounds after a year in the field. I was lucky out in the field and I was also lucky to be out of the field a few times when my platoon was not so lucky. I did carry some baggage home with me that I was not even fully aware of until I found the letters. The baggage did not incapacitate or consume me. I had somehow been able to keep it in a box. I have never had nightmares or felt guilt about having fought in the war. I feel no anger or hatred toward the NVA or VC. They did what they were being asked to do by their country, for reasons they thought were the right reasons. I did the same.

My only regret is I didn't stay in touch with the guys I served with in Vietnam. I think we all just wanted or needed to keep everything that happened in Vietnam in the box, so we went our own ways and didn't look back. Forty years later Davis' wife found me on the internet and we reconnected and remain good friends. I also found the phone number for Wagner and we talked by phone many times. We reminisce but we don't tell war stories. We don't need to; we lived it together.

From my conversation with Wagner, I connected with Joe Lux who was also in Alpha Company and we had an amazing phone call. He was wounded the same day as Wagner and they were together at the time. The stories Wagner and Lux told me about the injuries they sustained and their recuperation and the lasting issues they have had to deal with have really stayed with me. What they and so many others gave for their country is not measurable.

I have also connected with many of the Manchus through the 4/9 Infantry Manchu Association. The association runs annual reunions and I attended one of the reunions and got to know many Manchus I did not know and reacquainted with many I knew but had less contact with while during my tour. The group also maintains a website, as well as a Facebook group page, to share information and activities. They have sponsored trips to Washington to visit the Vietnam Memorial and return trips to Vietnam. They also organized many local events to share the Manchu history and stories. Many of the members and spouses devote significant time to

Afterword

the activities. And it has provided a forum for surviving spouses and family members to find out more about their loved ones. It is a really amazing group and I have thoroughly enjoyed the interaction. I regret that I have not attended more of the reunions and hope I can change that in the future. There are too many Manchus I have contact with to name, and I would certainly leave someone out, so I will not try. But the interaction is important to me and I value the friendships.

Several of the Manchus have written books and I have read them all (at least the ones I am aware of). I thoroughly enjoyed reading their stories. The books provide significant details of their time in Vietnam but also about their lives and the lives of other Manchus.[1]

I don't recall ever hearing about Agent Orange while I was in Vietnam. We did know that the U.S. Government was using a defoliant that was being sprayed from aircraft. Along the Cambodian border we often saw the aircraft flying low and spraying. There was no discussion of any issues with the defoliant, only that it was meant to increase the chance we could see the enemy from the air and reduce the ability for the enemy to evade detection.

Only upon my return to the states did I first hear of the effects of Agent Orange and the efforts of veterans and veterans' groups to get the government to provide care for the veterans and service members affected by it. At that point, some of the effects of exposure were showing up in veterans and in some cases, their families, but the long-term effects were still unknown.

In 1991, Congress passed the Agent Orange Act which instructed the Veterans Administration to treat specific medical conditions of Vietnam veterans as presumptively connected to Agent Orange. As of November 2021, the medical conditions of veterans impacted or resulting from exposure to Agent Orange include: AL amyloidosis, bladder cancer, chronic B-cell leukemias, chloracne, diabetes type 2, Hodgkin's disease, ischemic heart disease, multiple myeloma, non–Hodgkin's lymphoma, Parkinsonism, Parkinson's disease, peripheral neuropathy early onset, porphyria cutanea tarda, prostate cancer, respiratory cancers, and soft tissue sarcomas. Some of these diseases

Afterword

affected soldiers soon after leaving Vietnam; many took years to develop.

The area my battalion operated in, called Corp Tactical Zone III, had some of the most concentrated spraying, especially in 1968. Corp Tactical Zone III was located between Saigon and the Cambodian border, where the Ho Chi Minh Trail was used by the VC and NVA to move between North Vietnam and South Vietnam, traveling through Cambodia and Laos.

Over 20 million gallons of various defoliants, most of which were Agent Orange, were sprayed in Vietnam. The spraying affected U.S. military personnel on the ground as well as those involved in handling and spraying the chemical and the Vietnamese people and their crops.

When I returned to the states and learned of Agent Orange, I had no current symptoms and didn't worry about it much. However, at the age of 49, I developed ischemic heart disease and had the first of two major heart attacks. I developed insulin dependent diabetes immediately following the first heart attack. I suffer from bladder neuropathy that ultimately resulted in kidney failure. These conditions are all considered by the Veterans Administration as having resulted directly or indirectly from my exposure to Agent Orange. While these conditions have created some limitations for me, they have not stopped me from enjoying my life and family and I still consider myself very lucky.

My life hasn't always been easy. There have been plenty of difficult, very difficult, times. But I have tried to keep that promise I made to myself....

"If I live through this year in Vietnam, I am going to be the happiest guy alive for the rest of my life."

Reflections

Now that so many years have passed and I had the cathartic experience of writing this book, I think (or at least hope) I can look at my time in Vietnam objectively.

My biggest revelation in writing this book is that I could remember the situations where I was seconds from death as if they happened yesterday. I still can. And I can remember some of the fun times but mostly just in general. I have only very vague recollections of other firefights where I can somewhat recall situations like being pinned down in a rice paddy and getting gassed and being unable to move so we had to stay and endure the consequences of burning throats and eyes while continuing the firefight. I can also sort of remember being pinned down behind a three-foot berm and having gunships get confused as to who the enemy was and having them coming in for a strafing run along the side of the berm we were on. And us jumping over the berm only to be shot at by the enemy from the other side.

I can also vaguely recall hearing the pop pop of enemy mortar rounds and looking for the nearest foxhole. And I remember an ambush while I was platoon sergeant where we popped claymore mines on a group of VC along a path only to find out our guys had pulled too hard on the wires while unrolling them back to our location thereby causing the mines to flip up and fire straight up into the air when detonated. We could see the VC running away uninjured. Once I realized what had occurred I ordered the platoon to open fire, but of course our M-60s jammed. There are other vague memories but not clear enough to add to the story.

Reflections

Over the years I have also been surprised by some of the comments I received from friends or business associates when they found out I had been in Vietnam. An example is one business associate who told me he had a good friend who had been in the Vietnam War and said it wasn't really that dangerous or hard—that all they did was put their weapons on automatic and spray the bullets around and that scared off the enemy. So, he said to me, "I guess it was not so bad, right?" I just said that was not what I experienced and left it at that.

I am shocked by the issue of the jamming M-16s. The story of how that occurred and the length of time it took our military and political institutions to determine the real cause and fix it is nothing less than astonishing. The fact that our leaders blamed the soldiers and marines for the issue by claiming they were not properly cleaning their M-16s is even more disheartening. That is not what I witnessed and it was not the cause. From what I can discern, the primary cause was the U.S. Army leaderships' desire to continue a relationship with a supplier of bullets that did not make a bullet that fit the design of the original M-16. So instead of finding a new supplier or demanding the existing one make the appropriate bullets, the military establishment instead had the M-16 manufacturer change the design to accommodate the bullets made by the existing supplier.

How many men were wounded or killed over this is unknown and unknowable. Plus, there is no way to measure the emotional impact of sending a service member into combat knowing he is carrying a weapon that most likely will jam repeatedly. The only short-term fix was to pull back the bolt, remove the magazine, take out a cleaning rod, and ram the cleaning rod down the barrel to remove the spent casing and then reload, consisting of inserting a new magazine and releasing the bolt. How could we have expected our soldiers and marines to be effective with these weapons against a determined enemy, with far superior rifles in the AK-47, is beyond me.

I was also then, and remain so now, bewildered by some of the decisions that were made. So many times, we did not follow standard military protocol when approaching a potential ambush or firefight. We should have been using what is called fire and movement where

Reflections

one squad moves and the others provide covering fire. Why we did not do that more often has always puzzled me.

I also feel that the issue of not allowing NCOs or even young officers in the field to make battlefield changes to the battle plan was a hindrance to our success. How can it be that we find the enemy only to leave and go look for them someplace else where they will have the advantage of surprise only because that is the order? Orders should be made to change to suit the situation. I understand that after the Vietnam War experience a group of young West Point graduates got together and made recommendations to provide more latitude to our junior officers to make battlefield decisions and changes.

I also believe the effort by the U.S. Army to give as many new lieutenants combat experience as possible was a detriment to success. In my experience most lieutenants were on the line for about three to four months. Just about the time a lieutenant got to the point of being very effective, he was rotated to the rear to give another lieutenant the experience. There was also a high casualty rate among lieutenants. The rotation policy may have contributed to that.

I also realize there were many soldiers and marines that experienced many more sustained and bloody battles and hardships than I did. The regions of Vietnam were very different from the rice paddies and rivers of the Delta region to the mountains and valleys of the Central Highlands to the mountains and thick jungles of the DMZ (demilitarized zone) in the northern part of South Vietnam along the border with North Vietnam. Each region presented different challenges.

Finally, the entire process of sending young men to a foreign land with the goal of killing people, and hopefully not being killed themselves in the process, should be reserved for situations that are truly a national threat to our safety and independence. We say we are sending them to protect democracy. Maybe, but let's be sure that is what it is because what we are really doing is sending them to kill people.

Chapter Notes

Preface

1. National Archives (archives.gov), "Vietnam War U.S. Military Fatal Casualty Statistics."
2. National Archives (archives.gov), referenced to "Combat Area Casualty File of 11/93, and The Adjutant General's Center (TAGCEN) file of 1981."
3. "Hello Vietnam" written by Tom T. Hall, recorded by Johnny Wright in support of the Vietnam War, released November 3, 1965.
4. A.R. Moradi, J. Herlihy, G. Yasseri, M. Shahraray, S. Turner, and T. Dalgleish, "Specificity of Episodic and Semantic Aspects of Autobiographical Memory in Relation to Symptoms of Posttraumatic Stress Disorder (PTSD)," *Science Direct* 127 (2008): 645–653.

Chapter 1

1. "Yesterday" written by Paul McCartney, credited to Lennon-McCartney, recorded by the Beatles, released as a single in the United States in September 1965.
2. "For What It's Worth" written by Stephen Still, recorded by Buffalo Springfield on December 5, 1966, released as a single on December 23, 1966.
3. "San Francisco (Be Sure to Wear Flowers in Your Hair)" written by John Phillips, sung by Scott McKenzie, produced and released in May 1967.

Chapter 3

1. "Jody" is a fictional person who stays home and steals all the girls while the soldiers are off fighting the war. The term originally arose in working cadences sung by Black manual laborers in the decades preceding World War II. Jody Calls, U.S. Army Center of Miliary History, *history.army.mil*.
2. Lines from the cadence "I Got a Letter in the Mail." No copyright or authorship has been claimed and any works produced by the U.S. government are not held under copyright protection.
3. Viet Cong (VC) is slang for Vietnamese Communists, a term used by opposition forces (U.S. and South Vietnamese) to refer to the military arm of the National Liberation Front (NLF). The VC were southern communists operating under the same command structure as the NVA.
4. NVA is the name used by opposition forces (U.S. and South Vietnamese) to refer to the People Army of Vietnam (PAVN), the military arm of the Democratic Republic of Vietnam. The NVA were northern communists.
5. James H. Willbanks, *The Tet Offensive, A Concise History* (New York: Columbia University Press, 2007), pp. 157, 159; MFR, MACV, 5 April 1968, p. 5 (Abrams quote).

Chapter Notes

Chapter 4

1. The Viet Minh was short for the Viet Nam Doc Lop Dong Minh Hoi, or Vietnamese Allied, and was established by Ho Chi Minh before the end of World War II.

2. Bao Dai ("Keeper of Greatness") was the name taken by Nguyen Vinh Thuy when he became Emperor of Annam and Tonkin, protectorates of French Indochina (covering present-day central and northern Vietnam, respectively) from 1926 to 1945. He abdicated the throne in 1945 after the defeat of Japan in World War II and handed over power to the Viet Minh. He moved to Hong Kong but continued to have influence in Vietnam and with the French until 1949 when he returned and became chief of state of the State of Vietnam. Bao Dai was the son of Khai Dinh, emperor of Vietnam from 1916 to 1925. Although Khai Dinh advocated for an autonomous Vietnam with close collaboration with France, he was essentially a powerless puppet of France.

3. U.S. Naval History and Heritage Command, National Museum of the United States Navy, 1954–1955 "Vietnam (Operation Passage to Freedom)."

4. Marguerite Higgins, *Our Vietnam Nightmare* (New York: Harper & Row, 1965), 5.

5. Ibid., 173.

6. Defense University, Taylor Papers, Office of the Historian, Department of State, October 28, 1963, Document 222, Paragraph 2, Memorandum for the Record by the Joint Chiefs of Staff's Special Assistant for Counterinsurgency and Special Activities (Krulak), discussing "Report of the Special Study Mission to Southeast Asia (October 3–19, 1963)." House Report No. 893, November 7, 1963 with Representative Zablocki.

7. Ibid., Paragraph 2.

8. Telegram 292 from the Embassy in Vietnam to the Department of State, Saigon, August 26, 1963, prepared by Henry Cabot Lodge, Jr., reporting on his introduction to and private talk with Diem which last two hours and ten minutes. Department of State, Office of the Historian, Foreign Relations of the United States, 1961–1963, Volume III, Vietnam, January–August 1963.

9. JFK Library, "Vietnam, Diem, the Buddhist Crisis," jfklibrary.org.

10. Summarizing the events that led to the coup d'état, the Pentagon Papers conclude: "For the military coup d'état against Ngo Dinh Diem the U.S. must accept its share of responsibility. Beginning in August of 1963 we (the United States) variously authorized, sanctioned, and encouraged the coup efforts of the Vietnamese generals and offered full support of the successor government. In October we cut off aid to Diem in direct rebuff, giving a green light to the generals. We maintained clandestine contact with them throughout the planning and execution of the coup and sought to review their operational plans and proposed new government. Thus, as the nine-year rule of Diem came to a bloody end, our complicity in his overthrow heightened our responsibilities and our commitment in an essentially leaderless Vietnam." National Archives, *Pentagon Papers*, IV.B, Evolution of the War (26 vols.).

11. Marguerite Higgins, *Our Vietnam Nightmare* (New York: Harper & Row, 1965), 187.

12. Ibid., 302, attribution to an Australian journalist with communist sympathies.

13. Mark Moyer, *Triumph Forsaken, The Vietnam War, 1964–1965* (New York: Cambridge University Press, 200)6, 286; Political Bureau Resolution, November 1963, TTU, Pike Collection, Unit 6, box 1.

14. The U.S. Defense Department's National Security Agency had deliberately skewed intelligence to cause the president and his advisors to believe the second attack on the U.S. had been

Chapter Notes

carried out. Naval History and Heritage Command, Washington, D.C., United States Navy.

15. Line from "Hello Vietnam" written by Tom T. Hall, recorded by Johnny Wright in support of the Vietnam War, released November 3, 1965.

Chapter 5

1. Report of the Special Subcommittee on the M-16 Rifle Program of the Committee on Armed Services House of Representatives by the United States House of Representatives, October 10, 1967.

2. Otto Fuerbringer, ed., "Defense: Under Fire," *Time* 89, no. 23 (9 June 1967).

3. Report of the Special Subcommittee on the M-16 Rifle Program of the Committee on Armed Services House of Representatives by the United States House of Representatives, October 10, 1967, pp. 5322.

4. *Ibid.*, pp. 5323.
5. *Ibid.*, pp. 5324.
6. *Ibid.*, pp. 5326.

7. The AK-47 was a Soviet manufactured Kalashnikov semi-automatic weapon. The AK-47 was a fully automatic combat assault rifle and was the primary weapon used by communist forces in Vietnam. The AK-47 was exported to China and its variant, Type 56, was developed and produced in China, and ultimately exported to North Vietnam and used in battle against the United States and South Vietnam as well.

8. Report of the Special Subcommittee on the M-16 Rifle Program of the Committee on Armed Services House of Representatives by the United States House of Representatives, October 10, 1967, pp. 5327.

9. *Ibid.*, pp.5328.
10. *Ibid.*, pp. 5333.

11. Single base tubular grain gunpowder uses only one propellant, nitrocellulose. "Tubular" refers to the share of the granule produced.

12. In double-base ball propellant the fuel (nitrocellulose, a type of gunpowder) and oxidizer (nitroglycerin) are mixed on a molecular level (*Journal of Hazardous Materials* [2009]). "Ball" refers to the shape of the granule produced.

13. "One of the most essential unit procedures in propellant production is granulation. The granulation process transforms small fine or coarse particles into huge agglomerates known as granules. The granulation process converts the powders into free-flowing, dust free granules that are easier to compress, affecting propellant gain size." "The Granulation Methods of Double Base Propellant for Small Caliber Ammunition: A Review," *International Journal of Social Science Research and Review* 6, no. 1: 247–251.

14. Report of the Special Subcommittee on the M-16 Rifle Program of the Committee on Armed Services House of Representatives by the United States House of Representatives, October 10, 1967, pp. 5332.

15. *Ibid.*, pp. 5357.
16. *Ibid.*, pp. 5358.
17. *Ibid.*, pp. 5370.

Chapter 6

1. A fire support base is a temporary military facility established to provide fire support, usually to infantry units operating in areas that could not be reached from the infantry's permanent base camp. Fire support generally refers to artillery which can concentrate a high volume of fire on a critical target and within a fixed period of time (seconds rather than minutes). George Fielding Eliot, "Fire Support in Vietnam," *Ordnance* 51, no. 281 (March–April 1967): 470–473..

2. The following information regarding the ambush is based on interviews

of Manchus posted on the Manchu.org website and by author L.D. James, a Manchu assigned to Charlie Company soon after the ambush in *Unfortunate Sons*, ©2005 Cambridge Dent.

Chapter 8

1. National Archives, *Pentagon Papers*, IV.C, *Evolution of the War* (26 vols.). *Direct Action: The Johnson Commitments, 1964–1968* (16 vols.) 7. *Air War in the North: 1965–1968* (2 vols.) b. Volume II.

Chapter 9

1. Jack Gould, "A Negro in Vietnam," *New York Times*, December 3, 1967.
2. *Same Mud, Same Blood*, documentary, 1967, by NBC journalist Frank McGee.
3. Peter Levy, *The Great Uprising: Race Riots in Urban America During the 1960s* (Cambridge: Cambridge University Press, 2018).

Chapter 10

1. The compound 2-chlorobenzalmalononitrile, a cyanocarbon, the defining component of tear gas was developed by two American scientists named Corson ("C") and Stoughton ("S").
2. Recovery patrols are the final phase after a battle, when troops return to the location of the battle to recover equipment, and most importantly, the bodies of troops killed during the battle. Recovery patrols are solemn patrols.

Chapter 12

1. In Vietnam approximately 50 percent of U.S. Army personnel were administrative and logistical troops. These troops were responsible for procuring, maintaining, and distributing supplies, maintaining equipment and bases (including the kitchen), moving troops between bases, and administrative chores including all the paperwork. Approximately 25 percent of U.S. Army personnel were combat troops that provided direct support to combat maneuver forces, including artillery, air defense, assault helicopters, and military intelligence units, chemical corps, signal corps, and combat engineers. The remaining 25 percent of U.S. Army personnel were combat maneuver troops which included the infantry, airborne, mechanized, armored and armored cavalry units. Erik B. Villard, "Combat Operations, Staying the Course, October 1967 to September 1968," Center of Military History, United States Army, history.army.mil.
2. Republic F-105 Thunderchief supersonic fighter-bombers.
3. This strategy almost certainly emanates from the phrase "Keep your friends close, keep your enemies closer," often attributed to military strategist Sun Tzu, a Chinese miliary general born in 544 BC.
4. McDonnell Douglas F-4 Phantom II (supersonic jet interceptor and fighter-bomber aircraft).

Chapter 13

1. Erik B. Villard, "Combat Operations, Staying the Course, October 1967 to September 1968," Center of Military History, United States Army, p. 585, history.army.mil.
2. Hooch is a slang term used by American troops when referring to Vietnamese dwellings that looked like huts. These huts were usually made from woven banana leaves and they had straw or corrugated tin roofs. Some had metal sides too, made from sheets of tin or aluminum stamped with names of soft

Chapter Notes

drinks that were meant to be cut and molded into soda cans.

Chapter 15

1. Combat Operations After-Action Report Information for 4/9 INF 25, INF 116 AHC, B25 AVN 25 INF from 680606 to 680607, vhpa.org.
2. Carl von Clausewitz, *On War*, J.J. Graham translation of 1832, published in London in 1873, Book 8, Chapter 8.
3. *Ibid.*, Book 5, Chapter 5.
4. Gen. Harold K. Johnson, Army Chief of Staff, "Program for the Pacification and Long-Term Development of Vietnam" PROVN Study.

Chapter 21

1. The Kit Carson scouts were VC or NVA soldiers who had surrendered and joined the ARVN as intelligence scouts. They were call "Hoi Chanh Vien" by the South Vietnamese, which means something along the lines of "members who have returned to the righteous side." In September 1967 Gen. Westmoreland issued an order directing all infantry divisions in Vietnam to include a minimum of one hundred Kit Carson Scouts per division.

Chapter 22

1. The M-72 LAW (Light Anti-armor Weapon System) is a miniature and lightweight bazooka-type weapon which consists of a shoulder-held rocket and a launcher that was used against NVA bunkers. It is a line-of-sight weapon with a range of about 200 feet.

Afterword

1. Books written by Manchu members (that I have read) include *Unfortunate Sons* by L.D. James, *Mokane to Mole City* by Stanley J. Adams, *The Soul of a Warrior* by Tim Rezac, *An Unrelenting War* by Bob Goff, *Memories of a Manchu, Vietnam 1967–1968* by Ronald B. Beedy, and *Henchman's Light Rangers* by Todd P. Dexter.

Index

Abrams, Gen. Creighton 23, 110
Advanced Infantry Training 19, 24, 87
Agent Orange 63, 64, 166, 167
Air Force 26, 26, 41, 45, 67, 106, 127
AK-47 42, 90, 98, 99, 169
Alpha Company 45, 46, 48, 77, 101, 102, 103, 104, 106, 117, 129, 137, 151–153, 165
Ambassador (Henry Cabot) Lodge 36
American Forces Vietnam Network 120
American liberalism 111
AP Nam Thanh 48
Arlington National Cemetery 113
Armalite AR-15 40–43
Army Corp of Engineers 153
Army Inspector General 42
Army of the Republic of Vietnam (ARVN) 22, 41, 60, 107, 109, 110
Army Reserves 2
Army terminal 24, 25, 149
assassination 37, 57, 59, 111, 112
attrition warfare 101–103, 107, 109, 110
August Offensive 127–129
AWOL 124, 149

Bao Dai 32, 33
basic training 7, 11, 12, 19, 47, 163
Battle for Saigon 23
Battle of Dien Bien Phu 33
Battle of Hue 22
Battle of South Saigon 74
Battle of Western Saigon 74
Bedford Stuyvesant Restoration Project and Corporation 112
belt sander 10
Ben Hai River 31, 33
Ben Hoa Air Force Base 1, 26, 32, 36

Billboard 100 8
Black Virgin Mountain 129
body count 102, 107, 109, 117
boots 27, 28, 38, 50, 61, 69, 71
Bravo Company 48, 101–106, 151
brigade 45, 49, 60, 118, 119, 150
Broadway Christian Center 113
Brody, Terry 95
Bronze Star 94, 121, 130, 160
Brooklyn, New York 9–13, 15
Buddhism (Buddhists) 34, 35, 123
Buddhist Crisis 34
Buffalo Springfield 8

C rations 50, 69, 70
Cable 243 36
Cambodia 30, 31, 33, 45, 46, 51, 60, 64, 67, 73, 74, 85, 107, 108, 114, 116, 127, 137, 138, 146, 152, 153, 156, 166, 167
canteen 50, 65, 69, 84, 85
Catholicism (Catholics) 34, 54
CBS Evening News 24
Central Post Office 31
Charlie Company 45, 48, 49, 101, 152, 153
Charlie (Viet Cong) 52, 128, 146, 164
chemical warfare (chemical weapons) 63, 67
China 32, 33
Cholon 23
Civil Operations and Revolutionary Development Support 109
Civil Rights Act of 1964 54, 112
Clausewitz, Carl von 107, 109
Co Loa Armored Training Center 23
Coast Guard 2

Index

Cochinchina 31
Committee on Armed Services, House of Representatives, Ninetieth Congress 40
Confederate flags 59
Confucianism 35, 123
Congress 35, 37, 40, 43, 44, 81
Connecticut 7, 27, 149
CORDS 109, 110
Corps Tactical Zones 45, 46, 85, 108
coup d'etat (coup) 37
Courtland Avenue 15
CPA 164
Cronkite, Walter 3, 24, 112
CS gas 61–64
Cu Chi 30, 38, 71, 72, 73, 75, 144, 150, 161
Cuban Missile Crisis 111

Da Nang 22, 59
Dai Do 73
Dang Trong 31
Dau Tieng 114, 150, 152, 153
Davis, Sgt. 46, 47, 77, 91–94, 97, 99, 100, 115, 117, 120–122, 127–130, 134–135, 151–152 160, 165
deferments 2
Delta 31, 45, 46, 48, 108, 170
demilitarized zone (DMZ) 22, 45, 55, 73, 118, 170
Democratic Republic of Vietnam 32
dentist 27
Department of Defense 59
Department of the Army 42, 44; Inspector General 42
Depression 11
Detroit 8
Detroit Police Department 8
Diem, Ngo Dinh 33–37
disposition 109
Dong Ha corridor 73
double-base ball propellant 43, 44
draft 2, 6, 7, 47, 53, 62, 157, 160
DRV 32, 33
Duc, Thich Quang 34
Duc Hoa 77, 85, 95

Ellis Island 9
English Channel 11
entrenchment tool 50, 51

fatigues 12, 18, 26, 27, 50, 69, 75, 151, 161, 162
FBI 112
Felt, Adm. Harry D. 41
Ferguson, Freddy 120
First Indochina war 32, 33
flak jackets 50, 51, 70
floor scraper 10
FNG 26, 46, 47, 161, 162
Fort Dix 7, 18, 19, 68, 163
Fort Hood Texas 160, 163
Fort Jackson 19, 23, 24, 29, 30, 65
.45-caliber pistol 38
foxholes 16, 51, 168
France 11, 32, 33
French: colonial authority 31; colonial period 31; Protectorate 32; Union 32
French Fort 153

Garner 50, 51, 77–79
gas mask 50, 51, 61, 62, 65, 116
Geneva Conference (Accords) 33, 34
Geneva Protocol 62–64
Georgian Calendar 20
Gia Dinh Province 129, 130
giao thua 20
Giap, Vo Nguyen 32, 107
Go Vap 23, 101, 146; Logistical Area 23
Golden Gate Bridge 25
The Great Rebellion 8
Great Society 112
Gulf of Tonkin 37

Haight-Ashbury 8
Hale, Sgt. 154, 159
hand scraper 9
Hanoi 31, 32, 35, 55
Head Start and Education Reform 112
Herald Tribune 35
Hiebert 87–90, 92, 93, 160
Higgins, Marguerite 35, 37
Ho Bo woods 122
Ho Chi Minh 31, 32, 37
Ho Chi Minh Trail 35, 67, 73, 74, 85, 108, 167
Hoc Mon 47, 95, 118
Hoover, J. Edgar 112
Hotel de Ville 31
House of Trinh 31
Hue 22, 34, 110

Index

I-Corp 45, 46
"I Have a Dream" (speech) 58
II-Corps 45, 46, 114
III-Corps 46, 60, 85, 108
IV -Corps 46
Ichord, Richard 40
Independence Palace 23
Inner Realm 31
irritant gas 62, 118

Japanese 31
J.D. Wright Tech High School 16
Jody calls 19
Johnson, Lyndon B. 8, 37, 53–58, 108, 111, 112, 174
Johnson Administration 53, 55
Jordan, Richard 72

keeping them close 76
Kennedy, John F. 37
Kennedy, Robert F. 54, 109, 111–113
Khanh, Gen. Nguyen 37
Kit Carson scouts 140
Kitchen God 20
klicks 16
Krulak, Lt. Gen. Victor H. 35, 37, 165

Lai Thieu 101
Laos 33, 35, 45, 67, 74, 108, 167
Lewis, Sgt. Larry B. 84
listening posts 67
Long Bien 23, 26, 27
"Long Hot Summer" 8
Long-Range Reconnaissance 120
LP (Listening Post) 67, 68
lunar calendar 20
Lunar New Year 19
Lux, Joe 165

M-14 40, 41, 42
M-16 rifle 38, 73, 106, 135, 159; M-16A1, 73
M-60 59, 80, 91, 122, 153, 155
M-79 38, 39, 59, 70, 73
M-90 91, 92, 154
"M-1966 Jungle Boot" 27
Mafia 111
malaria tablet 30, 71, 157
Malaysia 35
The Mamas & the Papas 8

Manchus 45, 47–49, 75, 101, 102, 108, 114, 116, 119, 153, 166
March on Washington DC for Jobs and Freedom 58
Mazza's Confectionery Store 16
McCarthy, Eugene 54, 111
McGee, Frank 58, 59
McKenzie, Scott 8
McNamara, Robert S. 41
Meadows, Lt. 60–62, 73
Mearns, Gen. F.K. 131
medevac chopper 78, 79, 93, 103, 104
Medicare and Medicaid 54, 112
Mekong Delta 31, 46, 108
Mekong River 31, 46
Memphis, Tennessee 57, 113
Michalski 80, 81
Michigan National Guard 8
Military Sealift Transportation Service 33
Minh, Gen. Duong Van 36, 37
monsoon 65–67, 69, 71, 73
Morrow, Edward R. 37
Mount Everest 3

Nap Cat 123
Nap Tai 123
Nap Te 123
napalm 63, 64, 79, 80, 94
National Broadcasting Station 23
National Guard 1, 8
National Liberation Front of South Vietnam 34
National Security Council 37, 109
NATO standardization agreements 42
Naval Academy 6
New Jersey 7, 9, 10, 18
New York Times 34, 49
NFL 34
Nguyen Clan 31
Ninth Infantry Regiment 11
Normandy Invasion 11
North Vietnamese Politburo 37
Norway 9, 14
Notre Dame Cathedral 31

Oakland, California 24, 25, 149, 162
Omboy, Sgt. 138
116th Assault Helicopter Company 104
121st Signal Battalion 129

Index

Ong Tao 20
Opera House 31
Operation Passage to Freedom 33, 34
Operation Toan Thang "Complete Victory 60, 114, 115, 117, 119
order of battle 108, 109
Organization of the Joint Chiefs of Staff 35
Oxford, Mississippi 111

Park Slope 13
Parr, Lt. 138, 146, 148, 151, 156
Phillips, John 8
Phu Dong Artillery Training Center 23
Phu Lam 74
Phu Tho Racetrack 23
PRC 25 field radio 87
Purple Heart 12, 162
push-scraping 9

Quang Tri Province 31

RCA (riot control gas) 61
Red Cross 13
Remington Arms, Inc. 41
Republic of Vietnam 22, 23, 33, 34, 81, 160
rest & relaxation (R&R) 116, 118, 121, 124, 125, 132, 136
revenge squads 23
rice 31, 32, 46, 77; bowl 46; crops 31; dikes 71, 76, 91–93; paddies 16, 52, 76, 77, 83, 86, 97, 99, 119, 151, 168, 170
ROTC 2
Route 248 48, 101, 102, 104
RTO 77, 87, 88, 91, 138, 140, 141, 158

saddle up 50, 51, 77, 139
Sadler, Barry 120
Saigon River 23, 31, 86, 103
St. Matthew's-Emanuel Lutheran Church 13
salt tablets 30
Same Mud, Same Blood 58
San Francisco 8, 24, 25, 121, 149, 162
Saylor 46, 47, 67, 68, 75, 77–81, 85, 93, 94, 97–100, 115, 120, 121, 129, 131, 151
Secretary of Defense 41, 43
Secretary of the Army 41, 42
17th parallel 31, 33

short timers 18, 156, 158, 161, 162
Silver Star 81, 83, 96, 125, 131–133, 135, 160
single-base tubular grain 42
social liberalism 111
Song-Gianh River 31
South Carolina 19
South China Sea 31, 45, 46
Southern Christian Leadership Conference 58
Southern New England Telephone Company 5
Soviet Union 32, 33, 41
Special Capital Zone 45, 46
Special Subcommittee on the M-16 Assault Rifle Program 40
squad leader 38, 46, 87, 135, 137–139, 146, 147, 154, 156, 158, 159
Stamford, CT 15, 68, 160; Stamford Advocate 7, 133; Stamford High School 16; Stamford train station 7, 162
Stars and Stripes 30
Stills, Stephen 7
Strickland 91–94
"Summer of Love" 8

Tan Son Nhut 74, 86, 121, 136; Tan Son Nhut Airforce Base 23, 49, 74
Tao 34, 35
tat nien 20
Tay Ninh 30, 38, 47, 49–51, 59, 71, 114, 116, 117, 121, 125, 127–129, 131–133, 141, 146, 148, 150–152, 154, 155, 157–159, 161
tear gas 61–63, 88, 149, 174
Telegram from the Department of State to the Embassy in Vietnam 36
tet nien 20
Tet Offensive (Tet) 19–23, 26, 46, 47, 51, 53, 54, 60, 63, 74, 96, 108, 110, 112, 114, 127
Than Nghinh 124
Thieu, Pres. Nguyen Van 23
Thinh Ky 123
tidal flats 31
Tonkin 31, 37
Tropic Lightning 45
TWA 26, 121
25th Division 30, 130

Index

Twenty-Fifth Infantry Division 46, 60, 150
Twenty-Second Infantry 151
typhoons 66, 67

United Kingdom 33
U.S. Embassy in Saigon 20, 23, 36
U.S. Joint General Staff headquarters 23
U.S.M.C, Special Assistant for Counterinsurgency and Special Activities 35
U.S. Navy 33, 44, 96
University of Cape Town 113
University of Mississippi 112
University of Tennessee 163
urban renewal 112

Valley Stream 13, 15
Van Danh 123
Viet Minh 32–34, 37
Vietnamese Lunar Calendar 20
Vietnamese National Army 32
Vietnamese Navy Headquarters 23

Vildieu, Auguste Henri 31
Vineland, New Jersey 9

Wagner 46, 47, 49, 50, 52, 75, 91, 94, 120–122, 124, 125, 128, 134, 135, 144, 151, 152, 155, 156, 165
walking point 75, 76
War on Poverty 112
West Point 2
Westmoreland, Gen. William C. 22, 54, 107–110
Weyand, Lt. Gen. Frederick C. 46
Williams 77–79
Williamson, Gen. Ellis 131
Winchester lightweight high velocity military rifle 40, 41
Womble 91, 93, 94
World War II 12, 13, 31
Wright, Johnny 2

Zablocki, Rep. Clement J. 35
Zedong, Mao 32

www.ingramcontent.com/pod-product-compliance
Ingram Content Group UK Ltd.
Pitfield, Milton Keynes, MK11 3LW, UK
UKHW041527230325
456617UK00006B/20